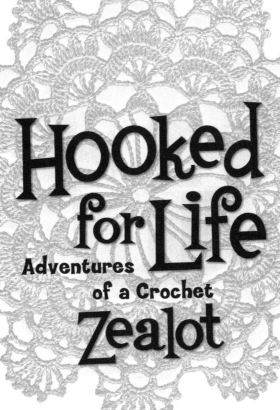

Hooked for Life

Adventures of a Crochet Zealot

Hooked for Life

Adventures of a Crochet Zealot

Mary Beth Temple

Andrews McMeel
Publishing, LLC

Kansas City

This one is for my mother, Doris McCabe, who put that first hook in my hand. Thanks, Mom.

09 10 11 12 13 MLT 10 9 8 7 6 5 4 3 2 1

ISBN-13: 978-0-7407-7812-4
ISBN-10: 0-7407-7812-9

Library of Congress Control Number: 2008936237
www.andrewsmcmeel.com

ATTENTION: SCHOOLS AND BUSINESSES

Andrews McMeel books are available at quantity discounts with bulk purchase for educational, business, or sales promotional use. For information, please write to: Special Sales Department, Andrews McMeel Publishing, LLC, 1130 Walnut Street, Kansas City, Missouri 64106.

Contents

Part One

Part Two

Links in the Chain Scarf 42

Part Three

Introduction

I learned to crochet when I was in the fifth grade. I wanted to make a granny square because my mother was making some for an afghan for the living room and it looked like fun. She gave me a skein of royal blue acrylic and a hook, and she showed me how to make those 3-dc shells. Having the attention span of a flea at that age (and actually I am not much better now), in the middle of round two I ran across the street with my hook and yarn to show my friends how cool I was. I sat on their porch and carefully finished the round—3 dc, ch 1, 3 dc in each space—and went on to work rounds three and four in the same manner.

Well, if you know how to make a granny square, and I have to assume that if you are reading this book you do, you know what happened. It got all oval and ruffly and didn't look like a granny square at all. That very day I was introduced to two very important concepts in crocheting. My neighbor Mrs. Gonzalez said that while it might not look like what I was expecting, it was still very nicely done so maybe I wasn't making a granny square after all but a doily—she was my early free-form influence. And then, my mother said I should rip it out and do it right—my first lesson in the importance of following the pattern if you want the project to look anything like the model. I ripped it out. Mrs. Gonzalez was fun but I had to live with my mother. But from that day forth, I really was Hooked for Life.

Writing this book was challenging in ways that I was not expecting. When I'd written my previous essays, I have to say they came very easily. (Please don't tell my editors this—I like to make it look difficult so they don't feel bad about paying me for my hard work.) My process for first-person work is almost always the same: I sit down and blather out a first draft of whatever story I want to tell, then I go back and do some paring and fiddling. By and large, if I can't dribble out a beginning, middle, and end in the first draft, the idea isn't quite ready for public consumption and I flit on to something else until it is.

This time, I made a list of things I wanted to write about, stories I wanted to tell, and I went to work. And when I went back and read over the early drafts, they weren't as clever as I had hoped. They weren't as glib, as funny as the other pieces. Some of them were downright angry—crocheters in general, and I in particular, can get so beaten down sometimes, feeling like the poor relation of our much hipper, trendier cousins, knitters. I wasn't mocking my crochet obsession as I did with my knitting one, but I was defending it. Which is maybe very noble, but doesn't make for a scintillating read.

So I decided this book would be a celebration of what crocheting is to those of us who love it. Not an apologia to those who do not understand, for they probably never will. Not a defense of crochet, for it needs no defending. Not a history of crochet, because although we sadly need one, I am not a scholar (if you want to know why, read the essay on how

I crocheted through school from eighth grade on). This book is a celebration of what is wonderful about the craft, nay, the art, of crochet. It includes a little half-cocked history, a sweet knowing smile at its foibles, and as always my tales of how my own life has been formed, row by row, round by round, by the work that I do. If you look down on crochet, put this book down. It isn't my job to change your mind. But if you love crochet as I do, or at least have a yarny open mind, please read on. There is more to honor than to scorn, and I welcome you on my journey.

Author's Note

Once upon a time, I wrote an essay that mentioned a doctor friend. I called him a vascular surgeon. After publication of the essay, he heatedly (although with a slight self-deprecating smile so I wouldn't panic) told me that he was board certified in internal medicine and vascular medicine, and as such, was not just a vascular surgeon as I had so glibly christened him. I pointed out that inserting his full title would have wreaked havoc with my sentence structure, and since it wasn't a medical book, he would need to get over it. He did. I think.

In the further interest of sentence structure, where a personal pronoun needed to be used to refer to a crocheter, I used she or her, not he or she, or his or her, or whatever gender-inclusive combination that would have fit. It's not that I don't know that there are male crocheters. It's not that I wanted to exclude the male readers of this book. It's just that I find that dual-gender language clunky and I wanted to avoid it, and crocheters by demographic are overwhelmingly female. Please don't hate me.

Pattern Abbreviations

beg – beginning

ch – chain

dc – double crochet

dc2tog – double crochet two together, a decrease. Yo, hook through st, yo draw through st, yo, draw through 2 loops on hook, yo, hook through next st, yo, draw through next st, yo, draw through 2 loops on hook, yo, draw through all 3 loops on hook.

rep – repeat

rnd – round

RS – right side

sc – single crochet

sk – skip

sl st – slip stitch

sp – space

t-ch – turning chain

Part One

Decorative Wristlets

Decorative as opposed to functional, these pretty linen wristlets definitely celebrate form over function. But why not make something simply pretty for your clever, hardworking hands? Wear them with jeans and a sweater, or with your suits for a quick yet work-appropriate hit of pretty.

Materials:

- 137 yards DK weight (CYCA 3, light) 100% linen yarn. Model shown used one skein of Fibra Natura Flax in color #04.
- Crochet hook size G/6/4 mm, or size needed to get gauge
- ½ yard ⅜-inch ivory satin ribbon, cut in half
- Coordinating sewing thread and needle to attach buttons and ribbons
- Four ⅜-inch ivory-colored shank buttons

Gauge: 9 sts and 4 rows = 2 inches in dc

Note: Ch-3 always counts as 1 dc, ch-4 counts as 1 dc plus a ch-1.

Ch 33.

Row 1 (RS): Dc in 4th ch from hook and in each ch across. Ch 3, turn. (31 dc, counting t-ch)

Row 2: Sk 1st dc, dc in each dc across. Ch 4, turn.

Row 3: Skip 2 dc, dc in next dc, *ch 1, sk 1 dc, dc in next dc. Repeat from * to end. Ch 3, turn. (15 ch-1 sp)

Row 4: Sk 1st dc, dc in each ch-1 sp and dc across to end. Ch 3, turn. (31 dc, counting beg-ch)

Row 5: Sk 1st dc, dc in each dc across. Ch 4, turn.

Row 6: Dc in 1st dc, *sk 1 dc, (dc, ch 1, dc) in next dc. Repeat from * to end. Ch 4, turn. (32 dc)

Row 7: Sk 1st dc, dc in ch-1 sp, *(ch 1, dc in next dc) 2 times, ch 1, dc in next ch-1 sp. Repeat from * to end, ch 1, dc in 3rd ch of t-ch. Ch 4, turn. (48 dcs)

Row 8: Sk 1st dc and ch-1 sp, dc in next dc, *ch 1, sk ch-1 sp, dc in next dc. Repeat from * to end, placing last dc in 3rd ch of ch-4. Ch 1, turn. (48 dc)

Row 9: Sl st in 1st dc, ch 2, sl st in 2nd ch from hook, *sl st in next ch-1 sp, ch 2, sl st in 2nd ch from hook, sl st in next dc, ch 2, sl st in 2nd ch from hook. Repeat from * to end, sl st in last dc. End off.

Fold the wristlet in half with the right sides facing and stitch the two sides of the ruffle (rows 5–9) together. Turn right side out before beginning row 10.

Row 10: With right sides facing, rep row 9 in the opposite side of the foundation ch. Do not end off.

Row 11 (button band and loops): Ch 1. Working down the wrist opening evenly spaced to the seam, 8 sc; working evenly spaced up the opposite side, 2 sc, ch 4 loosely, 3 sc, ch 4 loosely, 3 sc. End off.

Weave in the ends.

Thread one 9-inch piece of ribbon in and out of the ch-1 sps on row 3, stitching down with sewing thread at either end so the ends don't pull out.

Stitch two of the buttons onto the wristlet's button band, opposite the button loops.

Make a second wristlet to match the first.

A Brief
(and By No Means Complete)
History of Crochet

There is a fair amount of well-documented knitting history, with centuries-old fragments of knitted items on display at museums around the world. For crochet, not so much. You might think assembling a crochet history would be fairly easy. No matter whose theories you believe in regarding crochet's origins, it is generally agreed that crochet in its modern form is not nearly as old as knitting, and a shortish history should be easier to compile than a long one. At least that was what I thought, until I spent several days at a major research library, buried in the oldest crochet books and patterns I could find. Granted, I am not a scholar by training or inclination; however, as I make my living as a freelance writer, I know how to gather cogent facts. But the idea I concocted that I could dive into some crochet book from the 1840s and there would be an introduction that talked about crochet's history, turned out to be overly optimistic.

So I offer you the details of my research and some amusing bits and bobs I picked up along the way. Not to tell you that I have had a eureka moment and can provide you with a concise and witty history of the craft we love, but to share what I do know in the hopes that someone else will continue on where I left off, and that if nothing else, my search is an entertaining story.

One of the questions that has been burning in my brain, is why *isn't* there a popular, definitive history book on crochet? And while I am not one to politicize every area of my life, I can't help thinking that a lot of it hinges on my impression that in the days when each was new, knitting was something that men did and crocheting was something that women did. I found this quote that told me that I was not the only one to have this thought:

> *In all ages women may lament the ungallant silences of the historian. His pen is the record of sterner actions than are usually the vocation of the gentler sex, and it is only when fair individuals have been by extraneous circumstances thrown out, as it were, on the canvas of human affairs—when they have been forced into a publicity little consistent with their natural sphere—that they have become his theme. Consequently those domestic virtues which are woman's greatest pride, those retiring characteristics which are her most becoming ornament, those gentle occupations which are her best employment, find no record on pages whose chief aim and end is the blazoning of manly heroism, of royal disputations, or of trumpet-stirring records. And if this is the case even with historians of enlightened times, who have the gallantry to allow women to be a component part of creation, we can hardly wonder that in darker days she should be utterly and entirely overlooked.*
>
> —Mrs. Henry Owen, Countess of Wilton,
> *The Illuminated Book of Needlework*, 1847

The countess was talking about all sorts of needlework, not just crochet, but she does have a chapter on crochet in her book. No more tasty tidbits on its origins, though—I have to admit I was disappointed by that. I also had to note that while she lamented the lack of women's influence on history, her byline identified her as "Mrs. Henry Owen," not "whatever-the-countess's-first-name-happened-to-be Owen." The poor woman churns out hundreds of pages and gets her husband's name on the cover!

The earliest books on crochet I could find were printed in 1846 but the timing could be just as much due to the increasing ease of book production and printing at that time as it is with crochet's popularity. Meaning there weren't as many books on any subject printed prior to the mid-1830s—the process was just too expensive. Early patterns were short and sweet, and often did not have much in the way of illustration. Some of my very favorites showed a line drawing of a hook at the beginning and then instructed the reader to get a hook about the size of the one in the picture, or started a round by stating the crocheter should make a starting chain about this big and go on from there. I have always thought that crocheters in general were very visually oriented and now I wonder if that is because our patterns have always been visual instead of text heavy. I can only imagine the confusion at the local yarn store (LYS), however, if we all went in there with pictures of hooks and yarn and asked for those exact supplies——now if we could just all agree to go metric instead of U.S. number/U.S. letter/maybe the metric size—but that is another story.

So I am still hunting for crochet origins, and I find this:

*This pretty and useful fancy work first became fashionable
about the year 1838, although it was practiced in nunneries
as early as the sixteenth century. The stitch is so simple*

that anyone can learn to work it; it requires less care and attention in counting than knitting, and can be more easily taken out if wrong. At the same time, the finer kinds such as Irish point, raised rose, and Honiton crochet are almost as beautiful as lace, and demand much skill and patience.

> —*Knitting and Crochet: A Guide to the Use of the Needle and the Hook*, edited by Mrs. Croly, 1887. Note Mrs. Croly still doesn't have a first name, but at least it isn't her husband's!

Nineteenth-century crocheters were the spiritual ancestors of today's "threadies"—they made fine-gauge crochet in silk, cotton, and linen, especially lace patterns, to use as dress fronts and trimming for underclothes and fancy dresses. There is some speculation that the reason crochet developed when it did was because of the increasing availability of affordable commercially spun threads. Homespun threads are by their very nature a tad inconsistent in thickness, even when made by a spinner of exceptional skill. But since the ladies wanted lace that was both affordable and relatively quick to make, smooth consistent thread—and lots and lots of it—was absolutely necessary. Then, as now, several pattern books were sponsored by thread manufacturers to point out how wonderful their products were.

A lot of what we recognize today as nineteenth- and early twentieth-century crocheted lace is known as Irish crochet. Irish home workers (and eventually those from other countries) were taught to make beautiful crocheted lace out of individually made elements or "subjects," joined with a free-form sort of filet background into a dress front or collar, or other sort of fashionable garment piece. For many years, the purchaser of a piece of Irish crochet could not only stay in fashion but know that her purchase was helping a woman feed her family.

Lest we think that at least Irish crochet has a straightforward history, I went on to read:

Irish crochet did not originate in Ireland. A clever Frenchwoman of the last century, Mlle. Riego de la Blanchardière, succeeded in imitating, in crochet, the old Venetian Needle-Point Lace, and this was introduced into Ireland by some English ladies anxious to help the peasantry, impoverished by the potato famine of 1846. The cottagers not only learnt to make the new patterns, but added to them, and improved them, and, ever since, Irish crochet has been a valuable cottage industry in Ireland.

—Mary Card, *Book of Crochet, Number 3*, 1925

Ms. Card—at last boasting her own first name—went on to say, "The art has now been brought to perfection, and is practiced in perhaps every country of Europe, each adding something of grace, beauty, or ingenuity to the common fund of designs."

Mlle. Riego de la Blanchardière was not shy about taking credit for the invention of Irish crochet. In the introduction to her 1886 book *The Irish Lace Instructor* she writes:

I am but continuing what I did when the industry was first started, having aided them far more than is now generally known. For I may claim that all this class of work owes its origins to me [sic] *early books, as Crochet Lace did not exist before the publication of my first one on that subject, which appeared in 1846, about the time of the dreadful famine in Ireland. With the help I then gave, the poor of that country soon learnt my 'new lace' as it was then called;*

Schools and Classes were formed, many ladies of the highest
position then as now devoting their time to teaching and
selling the work, with so much energy and kind feeling that
the enterprise for a long time was a great benefit to those
who were, and still are, so much in need of assistance.

Mlle. was quite fond of the patronage of ladies of the highest position, and had a selection of letters that she included in her book just to prove she hobnobbed with the best of them.

Fashion for the body was primary, but then, as now, some crocheters spent most of their time crocheting fine fashions for their homes. Home decor items of the period were still light and airy: tray cloths, doilies, edgings for napkins and hand towels. Larger projects included curtains and valances, tablecloths, and bedspreads, all finely wrought in thread, and all taking up the kind of time that none of us seem to have anymore. I can't imagine squeezing in the amount of hours to crochet some of these lace pieces must have taken to make.

Wool crochet, or crochet with yarn, seems to have become popular in the early twentieth century. "Now that every grown-up is making woolly things, the little girl will want to be doing likewise," wrote Flora Klickmann, a popular and prolific needlecraft author of the time, in 1915. The 1925 edition of Weldon's *Book of Needlework* agrees:

Of late years there has been a great fashion for garments in crochet
of all sorts, and this fashion shows no sign at all of dying out.
Besides ties, shawls and dressing jackets, we now have children's
dresses and hats, and ladies' dresses, cloaks and coats and skirts
carried out in a variety of charming stitches, while the jumper
[British for "sweater"], *above all, maintains its supremacy.*

Crochet in wool gives a charming soft effect, and many crochet stitches look particularly well when carried out in this medium.

There were not a lot of photographs of garments on models in the early twentieth-century books I found, but one of them had a beautiful shot of a woman wearing what I would call a shrug. I was quite surprised as I thought this was a relatively recent clothing development, but there it was in black and white called a "hug-me-tight" in the caption. Wristlets in fine silk were also popular patterns—and I had thought the craze for fingerless gloves was a recent one, too!

The popularity of crocheting with yarn at this time also lead to the early days of crocheted afghans. The Depression fueled the afghan craze to some extent, as an afghan could be made up of scraps from other projects, and using every readily available material was a thrifty way to beautify your home when times were hard.

The separation of crochet and knitting does not seem to be much in evidence in its early days. Although I found several crochet books in the stacks, I found much more material in books on both crocheting and knitting, or about needlework in general. Ladies did all sorts of needlework, and several large nineteenth-century tomes provided instruction in knitting, crocheting, embroidery, needlepoint, and even macramé and tatting. In such books, knitting and crochet went hand in hand in several garments—I started seeing combination patterns for garments in yarn as early as 1915.

To crochet and knit during the 1940s was almost a patriotic act. Making garments instead of buying them during the textile-short years of WWII was much encouraged. The 1940s also brought us the pineapple craze. "Decorative as well as delightful, the pineapple is the all American favorite design," wrote Elizabeth L. Mathieson in *The Complete Book of*

Crochet in 1946. Grass-skirted maidens danced around in the illustrations for everything pineapple. I am guessing that the desire for pineapple patterns took root around the Hawaiian shirt craze that began in the 1930s, when Hollywood stars from Ginger Rogers to Bing Crosby wore their Hawaiian garb with style and panache.

Then, of course, came the 1960s and '70s, when it seems as if crocheted fashions took over the world overnight. Wildly colored shawls, skirts, and ponchos were seen on hippies and hipsters across the United States. This was a homegrown revolution—the flower child didn't want to buy her clothing from an impersonal store, she wanted to make it herself. Although looking back on some of those trends now, we might laugh . . . it seems sort of silly to talk about living off the land while crocheting with 100 percent acrylic in acid trip–inspired colors—I think the beginning of today's crochet pride can be seen during this era.

It might also have been the beginning of the divide between knitting and crocheting. Did those darned long-haired hippie-freak free love loud-clothing-wearing crocheters scare the knitters? I remember the craft magazines I found in my mother's closet had all sorts of projects in them, in a variety of techniques, knitting sharing photo spreads with crocheting and embroidery. Back then, such women's magazines as *Woman's Day* and *Family Circle* also published needlework patterns in every issue. My particular favorites were the ones showing the best-selling patterns to make for craft fairs and bazaars.

And speaking of craft fairs, crochet has often had an impact on the economy one way or another—from nineteenth-century bazaars for charity, to Irish crochet, to hippies in the '70s selling their wild creations at the local head shop, and right up to today's independent pattern publishers and Etsy.com sellers. The author of *Beeton's Bazaar* in 1898 had some advice for the sellers of crochet that still applies today:

*They should endeavor to sell as much as possible without
annoying people. To be teased and worried to buy irritates
most people, and does much harm to the cause. The medium
between persecution and diffidence must be aimed at,
and when attained, great results may be expected.*

Words to live by in the business of crochet!

What's coming next? Who knows? But I hope as crocheters live the history they are making, they take time to take notes. I don't want the rest of our history to disappear into the sands of time with its beginnings.

If It Exists, It Must Be Covered in Crochet

I do not know where, historically, the crocheter's deep-seated need to cover inanimate objects with crochet was born. It might have been during the Victorian era. Crochet's first big heyday occurred during a period of time in which home decor was fussy to the point of near-clutter, when there was a cover for anything from a leg of lamb to a table leg that had anything to do with any part of the body—anything at all that might in the longest stretch of the imagination be remotely considered carnal.

Tables had doilies, upholstered furniture had antimacassars, and cases and covers were made for everything from sewing needles to lingerie to items whose original purpose is shrouded in the mists of time. No surface left unadorned, no small item without its proper covering. The Victorian crocheter never ran out of projects to make for her home, which served the dual purpose of keeping her personal domain in style and showing off her accomplishments as a needlewoman.

I believe the toilet paper cover craze is the spiritual descendent of the Victorians. One couldn't possibly leave something as pedestrian as a roll of toilet paper out in the open for the world to see—how vulgar!—and yet it needs by its very nature to be close at hand. So cover it in crochet so that it is decorative as well as useful! Does toilet paper actually need to be covered to perform its function? No. Does it need to be protected from the elements by a thick coating of yarn? No. Does any crocheter anywhere actually think she can trick you into thinking that what you are looking at is really not a spare roll of toilet paper? Probably not. But it is there, and so it must be covered. Afghans, when you think about it, are just sofa or bed covers, right?

What amuses me to no end today is the enormous number of patterns available so that the crocheter can cover with crochet all of the electronic devices within a 500-yard range of her hook. IPod cozies, laptop cases, cell phone covers . . . we are now covering up items our Victorian ancestors never even dreamed of. I almost understand the electronics-covering rationale—a cell phone could in fact get dropped or scratched, and a crocheted cover might protect it from damage. But as fast as we blow through electronics, I have to think by the time your laptop gets scratched up due to lack of a crocheted cover, you will be ready to buy a new one anyway.

Makes one wonder what the crocheters of the future will be making covers for, doesn't it? I can pretty much guarantee they will be making covers for something . . .

Doily Mania

The lure of thread is powerful. For those who feel its call, there is nothing like it. You are the master of the tiny hook and the delicate thread; you can carry around a month's worth of crochet in the palm of your hand (unlike, say, an afghan junkie); you can use your crochet to beautify yourself and your home. And you will never be bored with your work because thread projects have endless stitch and pattern variations. I am not, by any stretch of the imagination, a threadie. I need my Finished Object (FO) gratification way quicker than a thread project can provide me with my limited threadie skills. What I don't quite get is the proliferation of doilies. Some of us, my friends, have what I might call a doily problem.

I think there is something inherently beautiful about the contrast of a delicate piece of crocheted lace against a polished wood surface. A doily centerpiece on a dark wood table? I am so there. The problem, for me, comes when the doilies proliferate—now there are two on the sideboard, one on each shelf of the glass-fronted china cabinet, and a few more on the table. Next thing you know, the doilies have marched into the living room—tacked with pins onto the backs and arms of all of the upholstered furniture.

At least this practice is rooted in purpose. In the olden days, fashionable men used a gooey substance called Macassar oil in their hair to give it gloss and sheen. It also gave the furniture a big old grease stain should someone so anointed lean back in his chair. So the chair doily, called *antimacassar* by the Victorians for just that reason, protected the furniture—it could be washed and freshened up much more easily than the upholstery could be.

The doilies-on-furniture craze lasted well past the era of Macassar oil, and I have noticed the look is sneaking back into the public eye. It is a very pretty, vintage/retro sort of look. But beware, you will be chasing those doilies all over the house because by and large your guests are not sitting in your chairs sipping tea and nibbling cucumber sandwiches—they are acting the way people in the new millennium act. The Victorian hostess didn't have to deal with folks throwing things at the television during an election year or the Super Bowl, kids running through the room to check in, or Cheetos dust. Unless you are planning on hot-gluing those lacy bad boys down, they are going to migrate.

Doilies can be very pretty in the bathroom, too—edging a shelf or under a soap dish. And heck, if you are doily crazed, pretty soon you are going to run out of flat surfaces to cover in the main rooms; you'll have to expand your search for an area that could benefit from a bit of lace. Just be on the lookout for those heathens in your household who might dry their hands or wipe off their makeup with the closest thing available, even if that thing is not a towel or a tissue. Until you nip that little issue in the bud, you will spend more time washing and blocking your doilies than crocheting new ones. However, if you have a doily addiction, this may be a good thing.

When all horizontal flat surfaces have been ornamented to the doily maker's satisfaction, it's time to cover the vertical flat surfaces, the walls. Intricate doilies can be framed in such a way that each and every perfectly executed stitch can be seen and admired, yet since they are framed you neither have to chase them around nor worry that someone will damage them. On the wall, the doily looks like what it is—a cunningly wrought piece of artwork. In fact, I often prefer doilies on the wall to ones hidden under other objets d'art. I get that doilies serve a useful purpose by protecting that highly polished wood from some object that might scratch it. But what makes me nuts is that if you place something like a candlestick on top of a six-inch doily, you can't see the pretty pattern in the center anymore. You spent many happy hours making a gorgeous lace circle, and all anyone can see is the scalloped border. I won't say that's a waste of time, because I know you had a good time making it. But if a piece of crochet is displayed, I want to see it, darn it!

When the wall space too becomes crowded, it might be time for a bigger house. If that is not an option, it might be time to switch to a bigger project that will take more time to complete. I hear that king-size thread bedspreads will soon be all the rage . . .

Crocheting for a Cause

What cause? Well, pretty much any cause. I do not know what it is in my nature that makes me react to any tragedy in the world by picking up my hook and some yarn and making something for someone somewhere, but I do know that I am far from alone in my reaction.

One thing that makes crochet such a natural fit for charitable giving is the speed with which you can make something useful. I made a chemo cap the other night for a local hospital that worked up so quickly it drew a few startled looks from the ladies at my Sit and Stitch night. "Didn't you just start that?" one of the other members asked. Yup, started it, screwed it up, ripped some out, finished the cap, and all in about an hour and a half.

Actually, if I may digress as I sometimes do into my half-cocked ideas about the history of crochet, there seems to have been a relationship between crochet and charitable giving practically since its inception.

I found a book printed in 1898 that taught the ladies how to run a charity bazaar or "fancy fair" to raise money for others.

The idea of organizing a bazaar in the occasion of subscribing to any charitable institution has become a great feature of the present age. It affords opportunities to many idle people of pleasantly exerting themselves, discovers and brings forward obscure talents, promotes intercourse and amusement, and frequently ensures most advantageous results.

In other words, crocheting for a cause gave otherwise idle hands purpose and meaning, and the money raised for a good cause went to, well, a good cause. The author went on to lament the preponderance of antimacassars, pincushions, and tennis aprons (whatever those are) and went on to propose almost four hundred pages of other items that could be crocheted or knitted or sewn or painted so they could be sold. There were hints on crocheted items from bookmarks to petticoats to baskets to rugs—anything for a buck, so long as that buck was going to the needy.

The potato famine in Ireland brought about a different sort of charitable endeavor. Women were encouraged not to crochet items for others, but to buy crocheted items made by women who would otherwise have little or no income of their own. The maker and the purchaser were joined across thousands of miles by the slenderest of threads—but connected nonetheless.

Contemporary crocheters make thousands of items for all sorts of charities—blankets for Project Linus and for pet shelters, warm hats and scarves for those who need them, clothing for hard-to-fit premature infants, soft hats for those who lose their hair due to the ravages of cancer and its treatment. You can make any sort of crocheted item that appeals to you and find someone, somewhere, who needs it—you get the pleasure of your craft and of doing for others, and the recipient knows not only the warmth of the item but the warm feelings it contains. In this transaction the human element is as important as the fiber one—the maker has given from the heart as well as from the wallet, and the receiver knows that someone cares enough to make something for them with their own two hands.

Comfort, both physical and spiritual, is the name of the game for items crocheted for charity. Whether they are in the same room or on opposite sides of the country or planet, sometimes a group of people tied together by a crochet group online or in real life, get together to provide comfort to someone who has suffered a loss by making an afghan as a group project. Crochet is the perfect craft for a joint effort, because it is so much easier for each crocheter to make a square and send it to a central location for assembly than to pass a piece of knitting around and have everyone work a few rows. Like participants in the quilting bees of the past, we can come together and make the work of keeping people warm go more quickly. We take pleasure not just in knowing that our work will be appreciated, although that is a lovely feeling, but in the fact that we took care of business together. We draw strength and companionship from one another, and pour it into our work, until that comfortghan is positively vibrating with fond feelings. This finished project warms people from within and without, everyone who touches it, no matter what their role.

I once read a post on an online bulletin board in which a poster said that charity crochet was a stupid idea—a way for crocheters to pass off shoddy, second-rate goods and to pretend to themselves that they were doing good, when they should just write a check instead if they felt strongly about a cause. And that post still bothers me a few years later.

Obviously, the crocheter gets something positive out of making something for others, be it pride in stash reduction, learning a new technique, or making something fun to make that she might otherwise not have a use for. We all love to crochet, and sometimes it's cool to have a socially acceptable reason to do it all the time. "Yes," you can say to the passer-by with the raised eyebrow, "I do crochet a lot, but look at all the preemie caps I made for the hospital!" Charity crochet can give us validation that we may not get otherwise, and that even the most militant of us sometimes need.

Just as obviously, there are times when a check is a better donation than an afghan. Although I wanted to make blankets for Hurricane Katrina victims, I knew that finding shelter and food was a more pressing need for most of those affected, so I sent a check first and made granny squares later.

But my crocheted items send a message that cold hard cash does not. They tell the recipients that someone cares about them. They provide warmth, both physical and emotional, because as everyone from Mr. Scrooge on down will tell you, money isn't everything. A trauma victim needs services, but he or she also needs, on a visceral level, personal connection.

Cash cannot replace love, but crochet is a pretty good substitute.

Afghans

Fashion for the female has always had a place in the development of the art of crochet. But crochet has also had a large role in the creation of fashions for the home. For many people who learn to crochet, their first project is not something to adorn their body but something that is more likely to adorn the family room sofa: an afghan.

I have been curious for some time about why an afghan is called an afghan. When I was small with limited knowledge about world citizens and their names, *afghan* meant a crocheted blanket, not a person from Afghanistan. The etymology of the word never meant much to me one way or the other.

As best I can tell, brightly colored fabric from the country of Afghanistan traveled home throughout the nineteenth century with various UK citizens that spent their time in the East. (Or getting kicked out of the East—check out the Anglo-Afghan Wars I, II, and III.) If you look at Afghani textiles from the late nineteenth and early twentieth centuries (coincidentally the time when interest in crochet was picking up steam), you will see large pieces of fabric with repeating motifs, some of which are square, with contrasting colors and textures. And in Europe these pieces were most often used as home decor, no matter what their original purpose was. Shawls and wall hangings doubled as throws, smaller pieces were used as cushion or tray covers; it is no great leap in logic to see an industrious crocheter at the turn of the last century replicating the parts she admired in the imported textile with her hook.

Soon crocheted afghans were all the rage. A clever crocheter could make something unique and lovely without ever having to leave her home country! And the word *afghan* came to represent any kind of crocheted blanket no matter how it was made or assembled, and people who had never given a thought to the country of Afghanistan wound up with afghans all over their homes.

I have noticed in recent years that many publications now refer to crocheted blankets as *throws* rather than *afghans*. I don't know if the term *afghan* has become politically incorrect, or if the switch is an attempt to modernize our shared crochet language—afghans turn into throws, granny squares into motifs. But I prefer historical language to hip, so I still make afghans . . . lots and lots of them, one piece or strip or section at a time.

It amazes me today that so many crocheters make so many afghans— afghan patterns are among the most popular books and downloads. There just can't be as many naked sofas and beds in the world as there are afghans being made. But then I look at my daughter with her two current favorites, and I get it. Afghans might be acquired during a specific point in your life, even birth! But they go with you from place to place, a little (or a large) marker of an earlier, perhaps simpler time.

When she was very small, my daughter picked out a pattern from a booklet and begged me to make her a ripple afghan in neon colors, with appliquéd lizards and cactus all over it. Of course I did it. In her mind, that blanket conjured up happy memories of a trip we made to Arizona—it was her desert afghan, and she loved it, even though the colors made me (and everyone else who watched me make it) cringe.

Five years later, her tastes are somewhat more refined (thank goodness), and that neon blanket doesn't match a darn thing in her recently redecorated room. But she won't take it off her bed. It isn't that she doesn't have a more color-coordinated bed cover, or that she really needs the blanket for heat, it's that it contains not only my love for her in a general way, but a specific set of memories that she treasures. I can see that blanket getting packed for college and then for her first apartment—its worth to her far more important than its utility.

The other afghan she keeps near was made for her by my mother, who spent hours and hours working traditional granny squares like the ones that inspired me to learn to crochet so many years ago. Despite suffering from arthritis in her hands, my mother wanted to make something for my daughter so that her granddaughter would always have some Mom-mom love close to hand when she needed it. When my daughter is sad or injured or sick with a cold, that Mom-mom blanket is never far away. An afghan can be a woolly hug—and who in the world can't use more hugs?

Edging Your Way Along

A lot of crochet projects in the earlier part of the twentieth century were not completely crocheted, but involved crocheting an edging onto something else. Hankies were a big hit to edge—even with the most delicate hook and thread, you could get one finished in a pretty short amount of time. And no self-respecting lady would be caught dead without a hankie. I suspect prettily edged hankies made great gifts, too. In the days when I was scouring estates to find vintage linens to sell, I found the best collections of handkerchiefs in homes that belonged to teachers or nurses, perhaps because they received many of these foldable tokens of esteem during a career of giving service to others.

Sheets and pillowcases received their share of edging treatments, sometimes with deep crocheted lace borders in white or cream, other times with brightly colored edgings to go with embroidered flowers or scenes. There was a time when Southern belles in their crinolines were very popular on pillowcases—maybe to match the bed doll and the toilet paper cover as well? I don't know how Southern belle got to be a decorating style—I think the movie version of *Gone With the Wind* may have a lot to answer for.

It was a short hop along the linen closet from the sheet shelf to the towel shelf. Delicate woven linen hand towels had lacy borders attached, and even terry-cloth towels could do with a decorative edging in heavier thread.

My favorite towel edging treatment brings back memories of my childhood. My mother's friend Laurie cut terry-cloth kitchen towels in half, tacked down the cut edge with blanket stitch, and crocheted handy-dandy little handles on them that you could fold through the handle of your refrigerator or stove and fasten with a button, so the towel was always where you needed it. Laurie was quite fond of making these and we had some for every season—orange and brown on a Thanksgiving towel in the fall, red and green on a Christmas towel, and so on. The changing of the fridge towel heralded the coming of a new season in our house!

Edgings are really popular today. It is quite stylish to put a crocheted edge on just about anything from a garment to all sorts of linens, hankies, and felted items. Just stay away from the crinoline girls—they tend to spread and take over a home's decor when you aren't looking.

I think edgings are serving another, broader purpose in our time. A lot of knitters are learning to crochet so they can finish off their knits. The more they wind up with a hook in their hand, the more converts we will have to the art of crochet! Mwa ha ha ha ha . . .

Everything Old Is New Again—
the Toilet Paper Roll Cover

I don't know why toilet paper covers get such a bad rap. On the surface they seem like such a great idea—everyone has a spare roll stashed somewhere in the bathroom, and you don't just want it laying there on the back of the tank as if you brought it home from the grocery store and forgot to put it away. So why not cover it in some pretty crochet so it looks like decor rather than something you dropped?

Except it seems like many anticrochet types use toilet paper roll covers as Exhibit A in their list of reasons why crochet stinks. I think the real culprit is not toilet paper covers in general, but those that look like dolls in particular. It was a trend that all of us of a certain age are familiar with—not only did our mothers have one (or more) in our bathrooms, but every house we visited had one, too. Some of them had actual plastic doll parts in the middle, complete with female proportions not found in nature, sticky-feeling hair that can never be untangled, and glassy eyes that sort of stared at you unblinkingly.

It was bad enough when they were just sitting there being decorative, but the worst thing was when you wound up actually needing the spare toilet paper roll and had to practically dismember a Southern belle to get to it. If you thought it was looking at you before, you really thought you were getting some nasty glares when you reached up under its skirt and yanked its oddly truncated body (the plastic parts were all pretty much torso on up, as I recall in my nightmares) out of the cardboard tube. And then what did you do with it? Put its desiccated form back on the tank or the shelf that it formerly occupied? Take it to your hostess and mention that it needed a refill? Emily Post did not cover in any of her columns the etiquette of rifling through a toilet paper–stuffed doll.

Many years past the heyday of the covered TP, contemporary crocheters seem to be taking back the form, making interesting, witty patterns to hide the toilet paper instead of relying solely on the old ones. I am particularly fond of one found on the Internet that looks like a sushi roll! If we celebrate what others mock, we take away their weapons. The spare roll still has to go somewhere, doesn't it? And within reach of the seat seems to me to be a fine idea compared to the darkest reaches of the hall closet, for obvious reasons. I think I feel a new project coming on . . .

How to Get Gauge

Gauge, or tension, is the fine art of making sure you get the same number of stitches and rows per inch as the designer did. If she got four double crochets to the inch and you are getting three or five (or two or seven), you are going to have some serious sizing issues. And size matters. Even for a scarf, you don't want something to turn out to be 3 inches wide if you had intended it to be 6 inches, or 18 inches wide, either, for that matter. Don't ask me how I know, let's just say I have some personal experience with the "you don't need to worry about gauge on scarves" school of thought. My personal experience is two feet wide and nine feet long, and despite the fact that I am a tall person, when I wear this scarf—and I do—I need to arrange it artfully lest I look like I am being devoured by blue merino.

If you are getting more stitches and rows to the inch than you should, you need to go up in hook size until you get where you need to be. If you are getting less stitches or rows to the inch, you need to go down a hook size or more. Or sometimes, it's the yarn substitution you made that is throwing you—you might need a thicker or thinner yarn to obtain the right gauge. Or the needle material—metal is slipperier than bamboo and switching from one to the other can change your gauge. Or if you are happy with your crocheted fabric, you can redo all the math in the pattern to make it work out for the gauge you are happy with, or go up or down a size from what you would normally make to accommodate the difference. Or you could do one of these two things:

For tight crocheters: Just add water. Fermented water, that is—a glass of wine or three or a couple of beers is bound to loosen up a too-tight gauge. Just make sure you knock back a few each time you want to crochet or your gauge will be inconsistent throughout the project. This technique might interfere with an accurate stitch count, but hey, we are talking about gauge here.

For loose crocheters: Watch the evening news, call your least favorite relative, or do your income taxes. All of these are likely to make you at least a little tense, and you will tighten up a loosey-goosey gauge in no time. Alternate these activities with other guaranteed stress producers throughout and not only will your gauge be right on, you will be so happy to sit down and crochet instead of doing anything else that you will get a lot of crocheting done in no time.

See? Gauge is important, but there are many techniques available to you to help you achieve your goals.

Oh and I forgot one more—check for pattern errata. There may have been a misprint in the stated gauge, yarn weight, or hook size. Oops . . .

Crochet and Beverages—
Mix with Caution!

Even being the up-with-crochet type of person that I am, there are certain items that cause me to wonder what exactly the crocheter was thinking when she thought making this was the best use of her leisure time. Beer-can hats come to mind. Come on, you've all seen them—there are even some fine folks out there making new patterns up for them. Someone thought it was a great idea to cut the fronts of beer cans out, poke some holes around the edges, crochet around them, and then join them into a fun and frivolous hat to wear in public. And then, instead of running in horror, many thousands of other crocheters said, "Hey, that's a swell idea! I want to make one too!" And a fad was born.

Now, there are all sorts of fads I wish I could wipe from my memory: pet rocks, shoulder pads that made you look like a linebacker, neon-colored clothing for anyone past the age of five. But the beer-can hat has haunted generations of crocheters with the mockery it has attracted.

Many awful fads fade gently into the mists of time and better taste; however, the beer-can hat, like a zombie in a sci-fi flick, just won't die.

As for the first designer, I can only assume that she consumed in rapid order the number of beers she used in the hat. She was sitting there with her crocheting, a little soused, and thought, "I could totally crochet around those and it would be SO cool! Honey, get the tin snips—I'm going in!" She must have sobered up eventually, so why did she share her idea with the world? And why on earth did the world respond with hearty approbation?

Perhaps the beer-can hats were a subtle form of revenge. The crocheter wasn't the beer drinker in the household but wanted to get one over on the person who was. "I'll just turn these empties into a craft project and shame my husband/daughter/best friend into wearing it to the football game. They will look even more like idiots than they already do after a six-pack, and I will be able to laugh quietly in the corner. Especially when they tell me how stupid I look crocheting in public." This sounds more like the devious crocheters I know.

Beer-can hats were not the first fad that combined crochet and beverage consumption. Coming, I suppose, from the same instinct that brought us toilet paper roll covers and combined with the thrifty crocheter's desire to use anything and every possible material in her crochet, I give you the soda-bottle-cap trivet. The idea was to individually cover a handful of soda caps with a cover of crochet in purple variegated thread, sew them all together in a bunch-of-grape-like configuration, tack on a few thread leaves in green at the top and—voilà!—a delightful item to place on your kitchen table to protect it from hot serving dishes.

You can't blame this fad on the contents of the bottles—I don't think people get drunk from soda consumption. Perhaps the creators were nipping into the vino instead of the grape Nehi. And while I know the metal bottle caps were supposed to keep the heat from damaging the table, I am not exactly sure how anyone thought having scratchy ridged metal poking through the thread was not going to scratch the table, especially with ten pounds of cast iron and chili sitting on top of them. But this fad, too, swept the world of crochet—I can't tell you how many of these grapey trivets I found in my estate sale–stalking days.

Today, there is a bit of a fad for crocheted coffee cozies. Instead of using the paper cup holder from the coffee shop or deli, you crochet a thick ring of fiber to wrap snugly around your to-go cup, where it will protect your fingers from the heat. I love these from an environmental standpoint—it has to be better to have a reusable finger protection device than to throw one away every day, and they are a great way to use up scraps that might otherwise get thrown away (if you are one of those people who can throw out yarn). But as a crochet project, I find them a little disappointing. By the time I get going and sit back to relax and get in my crochet zone, I am finished with it. At least I don't think crocheted coffee cozies are going to embarrass us to future generations, unlike the beer-can hats.

Felting

Felting (or more properly in many instances, fulling) is the process by which heat, soap, water, and agitation turn loosey-goosey crochet (provided it is made with a minimum of 70 percent animal fiber) into dense wooly goodness. Unless, of course, felting is the horrible thing that happens to you (and more likely the non-fiber-literate person in your household who also does the laundry) when the washing instructions are ignored or your favorite 100 percent wool item is accidentally thrown into the washing machine with the jeans or towels.

If you have never tried a felted project before, I highly recommend it. It's a lot of fun to cruise along crocheting at the speed of light (big hook, big stitches), weave in the ends in the most sloppy way possible (because, after all, they will felt in anyway), and not worry too much about gauge or shape (because any minor fudges will all come out in the wash, as they say). You wind up with a flimsy sort of oddly shaped something if you are making a purse or bag, or a garment that would fit you and three of your closest friends. Then you throw it in the washing machine, do your thing, and it comes out looking exactly like you wanted it to.

Well, more or less. Felting is more of an art than a science—your results may vary. My results vary, too. Every time I felt something, I have all these grandiose ideas that measuring and swatching and testing ahead of time will tell me exactly what I am going to pull out of the washing machine, and yet I am always surprised (sometimes pleasantly, sometimes not) by the results.

The great news about felted fabric is that whatever you end up with will be acceptable in one form or another. As long as you are a flexible type of person, that is. I designed a felted purse pattern recently that had absolutely no relationship whatsoever after it came out of the washing machine to the sketch I had made. No resemblance whatsoever. It was funny and scary at the same time how wrongly I'd guessed about how the piece would change shape while it was felting. That said, I changed the title, did a little fiddling with the way the closures were set, put the original sketch through the paper shredder so no one would know how very wrong I was, and sold the design anyway. It may not have been what I expected, but it was still a pretty cool purse.

If your felted piece comes out from the wash and you simply can't stand it, the very good news is that you can cut it up with a pair of sharp scissors and make it into something else. Unlike woven fabric it won't fray, so cut away. Stitch the pieces into something else, throw a blanket stitch edging on, and crochet around it. If all else fails, cut it into 4-inch squares and call them coasters and act as if that's what you meant to do all along. No one will ever know!

I started on the slippery path to felting addiction with knitted pieces. They worked out fine, and one Christmas everyone in my family (who would appreciate them) got felted slippers. But then I started thinking about felting in crochet. Crochet has a structural quality to begin with so you can easily make all kinds of shapes. Crochet goes really really really fast so you can get to the fun part, the actual felting, quickly. Crochet is a pretty dense fabric from the get-go, so you can get an extremely thick and cushy end result, or crochet with a finer gauge wool and get soft and flexible felted goodness. In other words, crocheted felting ROCKS.

Scrumble Fever

S*crumble* is a word that I thought was a typo when I first ran into it. In fact, as I am writing this, the computer *still* thinks it's a typo. It's the word for a building block of free-form crochet—you make a bunch of scrumbles containing any stitch or fiber you choose, made in whatever manner suits you, and then you join them together into something larger.

Start with a hook and some yarn and just work in whatever direction they take you—scrumbling is sort of like doodling, only with yarn instead of with pencil and paper. The glory of free-form crochet is that it can be anything you want it to be, even if you don't know what you want it to be when you begin. You can combine any sort of stitch and yarn and texture and go to town until you get bored with it, then instantly move onto something else. You'll know when it's finished; it will tell you. Then you make another and another, and eventually, out of the pile of disparate bits and bobs rises a finished piece. It could be anything from a wall hanging to a garment, and it will be completely unique—a piece of crochet art that no one in the world besides you could have made.

Crocheters talk a lot about whether they are process driven ("Just give me a hook and some yarn so I can crochet and I don't much care what comes out the other side") or result driven (they have a strong idea what they are going to make in what size with what yarn and they are going to make exactly what they envision). Free-form crochet is for people who really enjoy the process of crochet. Not that you can't get fantastic results—you really can make some striking pieces that are a delight to wear or display. But relaxing a bit on the planning side of crochet is likely to bring you the most creative results, if that makes any sense. If you let yourself be driven by the yarn and the hook and what they are telling you, you can do a little planning later on when you have a clearer idea of where you are headed. The process crocheter doesn't mind taking a few detours along the way since it's the journey that matters, and may even change the destination entirely if there is a pretty pathway leading her away from her original goal.

Of course, if you are shaking your head and looking askance at the idea of yarn and hooks speaking to you, perhaps free form is not your game. Some crocheters need the reassurance of a pattern—a road map, if you will, to get them where they are going.

Which isn't to say there is no planning in free form. If you want to wind up with something wearable in approximately your size, you need to do the math about how you want each garment piece to be shaped and measured, as compared to how large and what shape the pieces coming off of your hook actually are. Some free-formers work with paper or fabric templates—they mark out the shape of the pattern piece they need and arrange and rearrange the scrumbles until they have a layout that is both pleasing to the eye and the correct shape. Some "build" their pieces on a mannequin to get the flow and drape just right. The fantastic news about free form is—it is never ever wrong. It is only what you want, when you want it, if you wind up with a little section that needs to be filled in, all you need to do is whip out your hook and yarn and crochet a piece that fits.

Free form is like making a jigsaw puzzle at the same time that you are putting it together. At least you don't need to force any pieces to fit in! And it's an excellent excuse not just to build up stash ("Hey, I'll use that skein in something somewhere because it looks so nice next to some of my other skeins") but to use it up. Because one of the things a yarn can tell you is when it is gone—no pesky leftovers to put back in the box, just set yourself a challenge to use up this sparkly bit until there is no more.

It also doesn't matter what type of gauge you like to work in; you can turn your favorite techniques into free form. I have seen some gorgeous free-form garments in thread that look like their cousins in Irish crochet, and some wild and wooly outerwear that will stop traffic (in a good way!), and just about everything in between.

If you can take the plunge, free form can be the ultimate crochet adventure. And you never have to leave your chair.

Amigurumi

migurumi means "Beanie Baby" in Japanese. Okay, in fact it doesn't, although it is a Japanese word. It refers to small stuffed knitted or crocheted (but mostly crocheted, yay!) animals, or anthropomorphized inanimate objects.

Some cool, trendy crocheter who is way younger than me introduced me to the concept. I thought they were pretty cute, but what would you actually do with one, or a bunch? My daughter already has a population of stuffed animals rivaling that of a small city, does she really need more? How many of these little guys would I really want to make, anyway? And how many designs do there need to be?

The answers to these questions are apparently collect them, yes, none, and millions—because the ami craze has caught on all over. People collect amis they have made as well as amis others have made. Crocheters buy patterns and materials for them by the ton, and even buy the amis of certain fiber artists to add to their collection.

Me? I don't get it. I didn't get the whole Beanie Baby thing, either. Apparently I am not wired to fall in love with animals that don't come over and wag their tails when I call them. And since they aren't fiber bearing, either, I really don't have a lot of use for them.

What I do like about *amigurumi* is that they have turned a lot of people who are not otherwise crochet lovers, into crochet lovers. Some fiber council somewhere decided that statistically, a lot of people turn to crocheting when they or someone they know is expecting a child, because crocheted baby things are so lovely. I think a lot of people who are becoming caught up in the ami craze will learn to crochet just so they can add to their collections.

Once they have been assimilated, we will turn them into all-around crochet lovers. The *amigurumi* craze will pass someday—does anyone remember that Beanie Baby prices ran to the thousands of dollars, and now they are in the discount bin at the grocery store? And at least the *amigurumi* will always be cool because they were not mass-produced—each has a bit of individual character.

In the meantime, someone hand me a hook and some yarn, please. I see a little lion that I might not be able to resist.

Part Two

Links in the Chain Scarf

Past, present, future—all crocheters are linked together through our love of the craft. Make as many links as you like out of animal fiber yarn and felt away!

Materials:

- 125 yards each in two colors of bulky, feltable yarn (CYCA 5, bulky). Model shown used two skeins Lamb's Pride Bulky, 85% wool/15% mohair, one in Rosado Rose #M183, and one in Raspberry #M83. You can also go crazy with feltable scraps—this would make a great stash-busting project!
- Crochet hook size N/13/9 mm, or larger. Gauge not important but you want a loosey-goosey fabric so it felts nicely.

Make one link, then for each one that follows slip the ch through the preceding link before you sl st it into a ring.

Make as many or as few as you like—I did eleven, and wound up with a finished size of 2 inches wide by about 75 inches long.

The tighter your foundation chain, the more ruffly your links will be—if you want flat links, you will have to chain VERY loosely, but I like how they ruffle a bit with a normal tension, so I didn't get crazy.

Link Pattern:

Ch 36 loosely and join with sl st to form a ring, being careful not to twist the ch.

Rnd 1: Ch 3, dc in each ch around, join with sl st to top of beg ch. (36 dc, counting beg-ch).

Rnds 2 and 3: Ch 3, sk 1st dc, dc in each dc around, join with sl st to top of beg-ch. End off after row 3.

To Felt the Scarf:

Felt the completed scarf by your preferred method. To felt in a top-loading washing machine, put the scarf in a zipped mesh bag and place in the washer with an old pair of jeans or two. Choose a small load size, the

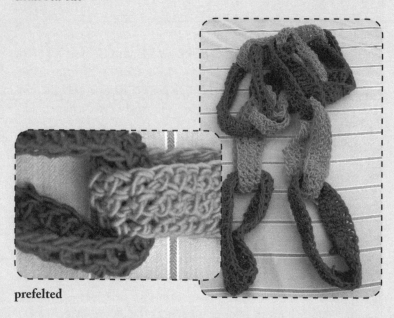

prefelted

hottest water setting, and the highest agitation setting if applicable, and add some detergent. Do *not* let your washer move on to the spin cycle. Check on the bag after ten minutes and then in five-minute intervals, resetting the machine as needed, continue the felting process until no stitch definition can be seen. Gently squeeze the excess water from the felted scarf, then blot it with a bath towel to remove as much water as possible. Pull the scarf into shape and let air-dry.

Greetings from Mount Yarn

There is an area in my living room where I like to sit and crochet, or knit, or spin, or sketch. My daughter calls this area Mount Yarn. If I am looking for something and stomping around the house with my searching face on, she will often call out, "Hey, have you looked in Mount Yarn?" She thinks she is funny . . . although sometimes she is right.

Yes, I have an office, but I find I don't always want to sit in there when I am working out a design. And I certainly don't want to sit in there when I could be watching bad television programs guilt-free because hey, the TV might be rotting my brain cells, but I am actually accomplishing something by crocheting, so I award myself a free pass to watch whatever goofy stuff I like. I couldn't watch anything serious or educational anyway—it would distract me from my crochet work. So bring on the sitcoms, I am working here.

Anyway, I have a light with a natural bulb, a small round end table, and a basket underneath it that is for whatever project I am working on at the moment. A large red leather armchair is my perch of choice, and there is a tapestry-covered ottoman in front of it. That is, I am pretty sure all of those things are there, but I haven't seen several of them in years. I believe there is an odd sort of magnetic force emanating from that corner of the living room that attracts fiber, paper, colored pencils, and crochet tools. No, not a magnet—a tractor beam. Okay, I don't exactly know what it is, but I know it's there because, at any given moment, there are twenty or thirty skeins of yarn, four or five stitch dictionaries, a stack of graph paper, two or three sketchbooks, a bunch of recent magazines, half the world's supply of Post-It notes (I like to play with Post-It notes!), and so many crochet hooks and knitting needles that the table top often looks like a porcupine.

Of course, when I am working on something new, or something with a deadline (like an imminent birth or major gift-giving holiday), or just something that excites me, the yarn, hook, needle, stitch marker, sketch pad, or pencil I need at the moment is nowhere to be found. It was in the pile yesterday. It might be in the pile yet, but I have no stinking idea where it is. After a cursory glance through the topmost layers of detritus, I usually give up and run to the store for backup supplies or move on to a different project.

About twice a year I get a burning desire to have that corner of the house look less like a dump site for homeless crochet projects and more like a place where a normal person would sit for an evening. After all, you can see that area from the entry hall, and I have on more than one occasion prayed that the mother dropping off or picking up a child is too busy to come all the way in the door, because if she turned her head ever so slightly to the right, she would see into the depths of fiber hell.

So then I clean it all up, relocate the "no chance of being worked on this month in my wildest dreams" projects back to the stash closet, file the magazines on the shelf where they belong, and throw out approximately two thousand yarn ends from finishing projects. Then I put all the hooks and needles back into their respective cases and discover that I have run to the store so many times since the last time I cleaned that I now own eight identical size H hooks. And so many tapestry needles (because I am *always* losing those) that I am afraid to count them all. But hey, I will never run out again, right? And look how pretty Mount Yarn looks! Hardly a mount at all, it's more like a gently swelling hillock.

This lasts for approximately forty-eight hours, by which time the invisible fiber/tool/paper tractor beam has kicked in, and the pile has started to inexorably rise toward the ceiling again. I swear that I am not putting more things over there, yet there they are. Do they breed? I actually think yarn that breeds would be pretty cool, as well as a blessing to the budget, but I digress. Is there a wormhole leading from the stash closet to Mount Yarn? (See, I must have been watching sci-fi during my TV binge.) If you are a scientist who knows about these things, please drop me an e-mail. I am afraid someday I will get sucked in and never find my way out.

But what a way to go.

Speaking in Tongues

I f you watch medical shows on TV, or police procedurals, which are my weakness, you find out quickly that like-minded people speak in a language all their own. "CBC, chem 7, STAT!" or "Book that perp for felony murder!" I am not always exactly sure what all the words mean, but familiarity and context give me the general gist.

Crocheters have a language of their own as well. Some of it overlaps with what knitters say, some of it is completely different, and sometimes the words are the same but have different meanings or connotations. I have heard it said that England and the United States are two countries divided by a common language; I think the language of crochet and the language of knitting have the same sort of relationship.

I don't want to go on and on about language but since I lapse into crochet-speak so much in the course of this book, I thought a little detailed explanation might be in order. Herewith, a little primer—a translation, if you will, from crochet to English. That's American English, by the way, I still get confused by UK crochet-ish!

Voy a la tienda del hilado—wait, that's Spanish. I may not be multilingual but I have managed to find yarn in every country I have ever visited. By the way, that sentence means, "I am going to the yarn store." Learn it; you may need it someday.

"My WIPS are taking over my available stash storage—some of them are going to have to be frogged." In English, this means "My works-in-progress (meaning, loosely, anything that has a hook glommed onto it) have expanded beyond the capacity of the drawer (storage bin, guest room closet, second home) in which I store the yarn I have yet to use (and may never use because quite frankly I bought some of it because it was pretty/on sale/I was bored/all my friends were doing it), some of them are going to have to be ripped out (while I sob bitter tears over all the time I wasted on that ungrateful pile of fiber)."

See? The language of crochet is a sort of shorthand that expresses more succinctly the thoughts of the crocheter. Let's try another one.

"My dealer hooked me up and now I have a raging case of startitis. I am going to have to CIP to get through this pile, and maybe join a CAL or two," is shorthand for, "My local purveyor of fine fibers, who is so intimately acquainted with my personal tastes that she can make wonderfully appropriate suggestions as to what sorts of yarn I should buy, found me some enticing objects at a fair price (made me an offer I couldn't refuse/lowered the price on the sale bin detritus she was trying to get rid of to the point that I couldn't put it back) and I am so excited by my many purchases that I must immediately yet thoughtfully (Hah!) begin a number of new projects. I am going to have to Crochet in Public (on the bus/during lunch hour/waiting in the carpool/at the supermarket/no matter how much my muttering while counting stitches embarrasses my

offspring), and maybe join a Crochet-Along (in which many crocheters work on the same project at the same time and comment on it, ostensibly to give each other support but in actuality to make those who finish quickly feel superior and those who never finish at all yet another thing to berate themselves over) or two because the camaraderie (or mockery—much depends on the general tone of the group) makes the project go so much faster (if only to avoid FO envy—remember, FO means Finished Object, and I promise I will stop now)."

My, that was a long one, wasn't it? Thank goodness, we have our crochet language to help us shorten our sentences or we would never be quiet long enough to get any crocheting done!

One last example:

"No, I haven't started that sweater yet, I am still swatching to get gauge," loosely translates to, "Even though it is a fall sweater and November is rapidly approaching like an oncoming freight train, I am making annoying little square after annoying little square after annoying little square in my pattern stitch, using every freaking sized hook I own (including using two sizes on alternate rows because I am just that anal retentive) because I cannot for the life of me get anything remotely resembling the number of stitches per inch that the designer got, and if I can't solve this problem I am going to have a sweater to fit a three-year-old or the World's Tallest Man, when what I wanted was a woman's size medium. I think I am going back to afghans. And don't ask me again!"

As you spend more and more time in the crochet community, you, too, will pick up words to express your passion for crochet. And some of them you might actually be able to say in front of your children without fear that they will get in trouble for repeating them at school.

Crocheting in Public

*If a poll were taken on hobbies, crochet would be found among
the top five favorites. Certainly there are very few hobbies
you can take with you to luncheons, picnics, and Aunt Emma's
tea party . . . relaxing soothing and strictly non-strenuous,
crochet is a complete rest—cure to be taken in easy sittings.*
        —Elizabeth L. Mathieson, *The Complete Book of Crochet*, 1946

I am rarely without a hook and a ball of yarn within grabbing distance.
It's as if I have a wooly umbilical cord that will only let me get so far
away from the possibility of needlework, and I don't want to get too far
lest it snap and cut off some vital nutrients. Crochet, for me, is an ambu-
latory mood-altering substance that is both completely legal and unlikely
to spill and make a mess. No matter how long I am stuck in traffic, how
many people are in front of me in line, how late my daughter's class runs

leaving me stuck in the carpool lane, if I have something to crochet I am not wasting time. And therefore, I am less likely to want to murder whoever is responsible for the holdup. The world around me is a better place if I have some crocheting to do, both for me and for those I must interact with. Trust me on this, for I know it to be true.

I started bringing crochet projects to school during the middle school years and quickly discovered which teachers cared and which didn't. I am pretty sure I finished a poncho during eighth grade honors English—as long as my work was done and done well, Mr. Beckett didn't care what I did with the other parts of my brain. Mr. James, however, who taught social studies, was insistent that he required my full attention and my hands to be still. I disliked Mr. James fairly intently—until it turned out he was a needleworker, too. He sat in on my sewing class one day (I have no idea why) and taught me a cool trick for untangling threads during hand sewing. But I digress. Middle school gave me the guidelines for crocheting through my continuing education—prove you know your stuff, quietly bring out some needlework at an opportune time, and see if the professor freaks out or not. If s/he does, give up for a while and try again after midterms. If s/he doesn't, bonus!

But what about those joyous occasions that require almost constant interaction with those around you, whether you like it or not? Situations that are arguably less stressful, such as luncheons, picnics, and Aunt Emma's tea party? Madame Mathieson's advice aside, there are often places where I am just itching to get some quality time with my current work-in-progress but experience has taught me that whipping out the hook is going to cause me some grief. Weddings, religious services, school plays, dance recitals . . . while I understand that these events take on epic proportions in the minds of those most directly involved, honestly, the rest of us could probably get by with half of our attention elsewhere. And with a little fiber in hand, we could probably get more enjoyment out of the event, at that! But start double-crocheting away at one of these events and you are bound to attract the ire of a noncrafty attendee.

I am good at multitasking. I really will hear every word of the wedding vows even if I am making a sweater for the baby shower that I suspect is soon to follow. And in the unlikely event that I miss something, in this era of high technology there is bound to be a highlight reel available within forty-eight hours of the event.

Of course, part of the reason I know I can handle all this multitasking is that I am very careful to match my projects to the affair. I plan for large events by bringing appropriate WIPs—even in my finishing-hungry delirium, I know better than to bring to Little Junior's christening an entire throw or a lace pattern that requires me to count every row. But try explaining your considerate forethought to those around you who are firing you nasty "How could you?" looks. If it looks as if I am about to be strung up afterward by insulted parents and in-laws of those who are center stage, I usually cave in and put my crochet away—not because I think I am wrong, but because tea parties, like traffic jams, shall pass sooner rather than later. My crocheting will wait.

Sometimes just knowing I could crochet if I wanted to is enough to get me through an event. I may know ahead of time in my heart of hearts that there is no possible way I could work on my shawl during Great-Great-Uncle Whatsit's funeral without setting off World War III, or at the very least insulting a cousin or two whose feelings I would spare during this stressful time. But I'll tuck the hook and the skein in my purse anyway . . . purely in case of emergency. I keep a fifth of good vodka in the freezer for much the same reason—I rarely need it, but knowing it is there and ready for me when and if I do is a comforting thought.

Now, if only I could convince the nice lady at the gym that carrying around a pound of yarn that I know I won't use is aerobic in nature. The gym, of course, is a social situation that does not lend itself to crochet. But only because I don't want my yarn to get all sweaty or to entangle myself on the stair stepper to the point that I would need scissors to get away.

Crochet on the Runway

I have crocheted for years and years (and years, but I don't like to admit to that last group). Crochet has always been fashion driven—it was popularized to glam up ladies dresses with lacy goodness—but recently it seems to be taking over the runways from Milan to Paris to New York.

Now, I am not a big follower of fashion, as a brief glance at my wardrobe would attest. My daughter keeps threatening to put me on one of those television makeover shows, although could you imagine the bleeping if the host tried to throw out one of my crocheted tops? I suspect I would not be ladylike about that at all. But I do love paging through the fashion magazines—you know, the ones that are about the size of the New York phone book—and checking out all of the crochet.

Some of it is more than a little odd. I know fashion design is supposed to be pushing the envelope, but some of these things should have stayed sealed up. And I just know that thirty years from now, knitters will be still be mocking us—not for the granny-square shrink tops from the '70s but for some of the asymmetrical, oversized, randomly fitted "fashion" that is strolling down the catwalk today. And it won't be the average, everyday crocheter who will have been responsible for these atrocities; it will be a big-name designer.

Not that it's all awful, by any means. There are some Seventh Avenue designers doing wonders with crocheted lace and beautifully tailored pieces that fit like a dream. Sometimes when I want a laugh, though, I stop in at a high-end store and look at the prices on a crocheted jacket—they can run into the thousands of dollars. I laugh not because I don't think they are worth that—we all know the amount of time a beautifully finished garment can take so a few thousand dollars seems about right to me—but can you imagine what would happen if any of the thousands of crocheters who sell finished items tried to get those types of prices? There would be a panic in the shops! Because something tells me the maker of that sweater doesn't get nearly as much money as the person whose name is on the label.

Actually, as fashion styles trickle down through the price points, what bothers me is not the $3,000 sweater at Neiman Marcus but the $15 poncho at Target. Whoever made that crocheted garment, and if it is completely crocheted it was definitely a person not a machine, didn't get paid nearly enough money for her work. I understand that the cost of living in whatever country she lives in is not the same as in the United States, but she probably got an hourly rate that we could pay with pocket change. If we train consumers to shop a discount store for crocheted fashion, then when they run across someone selling a few pieces for a fair rate, the customers think they are overpriced.

Anyway, if fashion history tells us anything, it is that no one trend lasts for too long. If you like crocheting garments for family and friends to wear, quick, do some now while they are still in style. I have crocheted when it was in style and I have crocheted when it wasn't, so I know that we have to take advantage of our current stylistic cachet while it lasts. In a few years, only the crocheters will be wearing crocheted garments.

The Crochet Time Warp

I am an experienced crocheter—I have been doing it for decades. I should know how long it takes to make a stitch, a row, a sweater. Yet each and every time I set a firm deadline for a project I find I have underestimated the time I need to finish something by a rather large margin. If I say, "Yes, I can absolutely have that in the mail to you by Tuesday," and it happens to be Thursday, I can pretty much guarantee you that the only way that would be possible without breaking any of the laws of physics would be if I neither slept, nor ate, nor took potty breaks. Those first two I might manage, but the last is problematic . . .

I have been known to choose delivery services based on what time their lobby window closes rather than which one is cheaper or more reliable. For the record? The local UPS deadline is 1:00 P.M., the USPS is 5:00 P.M., and for those really desperate dashes, there is a FedEx a twenty-minute drive away that accepts packages until 8:30 P.M. You get a FedEx package from me, you can pretty much bet that I was weaving in ends until 8:29.

Recently, I had an afghan to finish, and the crochet time warp was already on my mind, so I did a little math. I looked at all the pieces I had done and wrote down which pieces were not finished. I was on public transportation and was starting a new section so at the end of my forty-minute ride, I counted how many rows I had finished. Twenty rows in forty minutes (okay, they were pretty narrow rows) equals two minutes per row, give or take. When I got to the subway, the next leg of my journey, I used the calculator on my cell phone to figure out how many rows were left to do (X rows times two minutes, plus X hours to assemble the pieces and X more hours to crochet on an edging). When I started, I was guessing it would take about ten hours to finish the afghan but the calculator told me it was a bare minimum of twenty-eight and a half hours if all went well. As it happens, it took me about thirty hours. Ten hours? Ha! I wasn't even close. Of course, how much crochet time did I have to comfortably make it to UPS? Twelve hours. Darn, FedEx again! And no sleep, and no meal breaks and—well you get the idea.

The other facet of the crochet time warp is that when I have my crochet mojo going, time passes and I am completely unaware of it. Same project, different day . . . I had the house to myself and a deadline to make, so I sat down in front of a crime show marathon on cable TV and started to crochet. The marathon started at noon. I was going to town on the afghan border and my stomach started to growl a little, so I thought I might take a break and go get some lunch. It was a little darker than I expected—was there a rainstorm blowing in? No, it was dusky and I was starving because it was six o'clock, not two, as I had thought. Where had the time gone? Lost in the crochet time warp.

As you can see, sometimes the crochet time warp is a bad thing (missed deadlines due to underestimation of time needed) and sometimes it is a good thing (blasting through a project without it feeling like work). What I think we need to do here is harness the power of the crochet time warp so that we can use its powers for good and not evil.

If only I could crochet through a root canal, those are some hours that I wish would flash by at the speed of light.

How Small Is Too Small?

To keep, I mean. We talk about stash taking over the world, and at least in this house, it does. But stash, to me, is mostly full skeins, or sometimes half skeins that go with other skeins—sizeable chunks of the same color and dye lot that I could conceivably use for a project with little to no trouble.

But then there are the other storage boxes—smaller than my regular stash storage boxes—that are labeled "odd balls and bits." I started collecting the smallish bits of leftovers to store in one of those boxes, and next thing you knew there were two boxes, then three. Frankly, there are a lot of wee little balls of yarn in this house that are leftovers from finished projects. And when I set out to find them on my last ill-advised attempt at yarn containment, I found many more than I bargained for. It seemed like a good idea to get rid of some of them, but I find it physically impossible to throw yarn away. So here they sit.

Sometimes I consciously start on a stash-busting sort of project that is specifically designed to use up the partial skeins I have lying around. But often times those projects call for small amounts of yarn that are still smaller than what I have lying around so I use some odd balls but I don't use them up. If there is anything more useless than a thirty-seven-yard ball of yarn, it is a seven-yard ball of yarn. But back in the box it goes, because I can't throw out yarn.

I donate a lot of yarn to a local senior citizens' center, but I don't want to give them the ratty little balls because I think that would be at least a little bit insulting. I want them to be happy when I come in holding garbage bags full of yarn, rather than thinking I am giving them actual garbage.

In perusing a knit and crochet publication put out by the *New York Herald Tribune* in the late 1940s, I saw directions for a crocheted, multi-colored afghan that began with the instruction, "Gather several lengths of worsted yarn *such as everyone has about the house,* and tie them together, winding them into a ball as you go." (Etc., and emphasis mine.) *Such as everyone has about the house* . . . then it's not just me, and it hasn't been just me for quite some time! Everyone has these yarn ends about the house—too small to use but too pretty to throw away.

Sadly, my other phobia in relation to this issue is knots. I hate weaving in two trillion ends, but I hate knots in my work even more. I nearly foamed at the mouth at a recent crochet and knit conference, when the class instructor told us to change yarns randomly by tying them together with a tight overhand knot, and trimming the ends close to the knot. Knots in my work? On purpose, no less? I did it because I am a good student (who did not really want to foment revolution in the classroom) but it made me crazy. It's making me a little bit crazy just now writing about it. So I am guessing that making my own Magic Ball, which is what many contemporary crocheters call these tied together yarns, is not the answer.

I decided that I had to have some standard—a firm mathematical concept that would guide my bits storage. If a ball of yarn has less than X yards remaining, it is no longer a ball of yarn, it is trash. I had to be able to think of something I could actually do with the yarn or it had to go. Of course it doesn't take a whole heck of a lot of yarn to do the first round or two of a granny square, so the smallish balls didn't really go anywhere but back in the box.

Recently I was finishing up a bunch of afghan models for a pattern book. I had left way long ends on the squares because I wasn't sure how I was going to assemble them, so I figured the ends would make good stitching-up yarn. It turned out that I didn't need a foot or more of yarn dangling in every color, so some colors I used to assemble and some ends I had to weave in, cutting off an eight- to twelve-inch tail when I was through. The tails started to pile up, and I had to do something with them. Had I finally reached my mathematical limit? Could I throw away a foot-long tail? I decided I could, and was heading off to the kitchen trash can when my daughter stuck her head in the doorway. "Hey, aren't those wool?" she asked. "You know, I could needlefelt with those, you should keep them." And then she went on her merry way.

I grabbed a ziptop plastic bag and threw them in, collecting more and more as I finished the afghan, until there were at least a hundred pieces in there. I looked, and I thought, and I pondered, and then I went to the trash can and threw them all away. Apparently I *had* found my limit and twelve inches was it. I was even good enough not to separate the longer tails from the shorter ones. I just threw caution to the wind and chucked the entire contents of the bag.

I am kind of hoping though that the seagulls and other nesting animals that hang out around the garbage dumps will snag these little woolen bits and take them home. Just think how soft and warm their nests would be. And then the strands would not have gone to waste. Maybe I should take up needlefelting . . .

No Brain Cells Required

I love all of the many forms my crocheting can take—from delicate lace made with a tiny hook and cobweb-weight cotton to a thick scarf made from bulky-weight wool. But sometimes when I am picking a project, I am less interested in what it's going to turn out to be than in how it fits into my available crafting time.

If I am home in my comfy corner chair with my special light on and every tool I could ever want on hand, the sky's the limit so far as technical challenge goes. There is something incredibly satisfying about working on a very complicated pattern and watching the results grow under my fingers. Even if I have to frog my efforts twelve times, that thirteenth time, when I win the battle of crocheter vs. crocheting, at least temporarily, can leave me grinning for days. And while I am working on the piece, I am totally involved in it . . . counting stitches and rows, working for hours to get an inch of fabric, trying to imagine how this puzzle piece is going to fit in with all the others and give me the end result that I want. My crocheting absorbs all of my attention—in fact, requires it, lest bad things happen.

But if I am out and about with only short spurts of time to crochet or in the company of people who are likely to want me to listen to them while they speak to me, I want brainless crochet. I want something that I could pretty much do blindfolded and standing on my head without messing anything up. In short, I want chimp work.

I cannot take credit for "chimp work" as a descriptive term, although I wish I could. I vividly remember the first time I heard it. It was the wee hours of the morning and I was working in the costume shop of a film shooting in New York City. There were two complicated garments yet to be finished, more to pack and ready for the shoot whose scheduled start time was mere hours away, and several of us were buzzing around like over-caffeinated bees trying to get everything finished while at the same time not making stupid, sleep-deprived mistakes. One of the assistant designers came over and asked if he could help. I raised an eyebrow—as a general rule on professional film sets, stitchers do not design and designers do not stitch. I wasn't quite sure how much help he could actually be—I had never seen him so much as thread a needle, and while I am sure he knew how to sew, he probably wasn't as practiced at whomping out garments as the rest of us who did it full-time. He blurted into the silence, "I didn't mean finish the dress, but I'll do chimp work if it helps." I fell apart laughing. "Chimp work" is such an expressive phrase that even if you have never heard it before you know exactly what it means: mindless, brainless repetitive work that someone with minimal skills can accomplish. I set him to putting a jillion decorative iron-on fabric pieces onto a garment that needed them and went back to stitching. Every few minutes I smiled to myself, watching him with the iron. Chimp work, indeed.

Chimp work is the opposite of mindful crocheting—it's what you do when your hands need to be busy but at least part of your brain is required elsewhere. Sock legs, scarves, and extra-large granny squares are great chimp work. Once you get going, you can have a conversation, look at the scenery, ponder higher mathematics, or the meaning of life— whatever else it is that needs to be done.

Now I have a sort of mental file of the available projects on hand, which ranges from chimp work through "I might have to look at this every few moments to make sure it is doing what I want it to do" on up to "If anyone so much as looks at me while I am in the middle of a row, I am going to lose my place and mess this up to a spectacular de- gree." What those projects turn out to be sometimes matters less than you might think.

Crocheting and Babies—
You Can't Have One without the Other

(Which doesn't mean I think that everyone in the world who crochets should run out and have a baby—plenty of babies out there would benefit from some crocheted cuteness, so don't feel the need to provide your own baby unless you were already inclined in that direction.)

When I talk to people who crochet, I always ask what got them started, and invariably the women and men who didn't learn as children became interested and sought out lessons when they or someone they knew was expecting a baby. There is something about a new baby that makes even noncrocheters (or as I prefer to call them, latent crocheters) rummage through pattern books and coo over blankies and bears.

Crocheted items are the perfect combination of utility and art, so far as babies are concerned. At the rate that infants leak out of one end or the other (or both), a parent or caretaker can never have too many blankets, bibs, or sweaters. Even if your crocheted offering is not an exact match to the adult recipient's taste or fashion sense, you will still wow them with the fact that you took the time to make something to welcome Junior into the world with your own two hands. And as for art—the pattern choices are almost endless, so you can choose something that shows off your particular skill set.

Another great thing about crocheted baby items is the speed with which they are finished—you can find out about a baby shower a few days before it happens and still show up with a lovely handmade gift that will wow the crowd and look like you were working on it for the duration of the pregnancy. That speedy finish time is also a great fix for those of you (okay, us) who like to bask in the warm glow of instant gratification from time to time. In fact, I know several crocheters who like to make baby items between larger projects, even when no new baby they know is on the horizon! Baby clothes can always be stored until their time of need, and they will always fit someone, so you can make whatever baby pattern appeals to you, resting easy that it will be used in time.

Although a lot of crocheters prefer blankets and home decor items to garments because blankets don't need to fit, garment sizing is a no-brainer for a baby as long as you don't make something infinitesimal. Babies grow really quickly, so if that adorable jacket doesn't fit Baby now, it will eventually and probably sooner rather than later. Any too-large gauge issues can be played off by telling the mother, "I know it's a little big now, but I thought you would get plenty of things in newborn size and that this would give Junior something to grow into." Not only will you not hear crap about your gauge issues, but you will also be commended for your thoughtfulness and preplanning abilities.

Blankets seem like the easiest thing to make, but believe it or not, you can really foul up a blanket with an incorrect gauge. When my sister was anticipating the birth of her first grandchild, she fell into the "I must crochet something for the baby" mode of thinking almost immediately. She chose a pattern for a set with matching blanket, jacket, and booties—there might have been a hat as well. She ran off to the store, got a soft, multicolored acrylic yarn, and started crocheting away on the blanket. She crocheted and crocheted and crocheted—and ran out of yarn, even though she had bought what the pattern said would be enough for the entire set. And she crocheted and crocheted and crocheted until the blanket was crib size. Finally, she ended it off and put on a delicate edging. She was so proud of all of her hard work as well as how quickly it was finished. She would be able to give it to her daughter well before the baby was born, even if she wound up giving her the garments later.

So, smiling and happy, Grandma-to-be presented her gift at the shower. First, the attendees wondered what could possibly be in the box because it was so darned heavy. I mean, this thing weighed a ton. We were thinking that it might be furniture that needed to be assembled, or baby books. My niece tore into the wrapping and pulled out the blanket—it really was beautiful, and we started to tell my sister what a great job she had done. But then someone (it might have been me) unsuccessfully stifled a laugh and said, "Well, as heavy as this is, you won't have to worry about the baby rolling off the couch if this is on top of her—she won't be able to move!" That got the rest of my family going (hey, I didn't get my snarky attitude from strangers). "Oh noooooooo, not the lead blanket. Mommy, I'll be good I promise!" came from one of my nieces. "Help . . . can't . . . move . . . arms . . ." came from another, and I am sad to report it went downhill from there. We had tears running down our cheeks from laughing so hard at the madness, and even my sister cracked a smile after getting over the shock of the first verbal assault (she, too, is a member of my family, so it couldn't have been a very big shock).

And a valuable lesson was learned by all, that gauge affects fabric density as well as size. To my sister's credit she went on to finish the garments, going up a couple of hook sizes now that she knew what the problem was. And the baby (now college age) got lots of use out of that set. After all, a blanket that densely constructed is extremely durable; it would probably survive a nuclear attack (which now that I think about it, someone pointed out, between snorts of laughter, at the shower). But I don't remember her making any more crocheted items for the rest of her grandkids—I don't know that she could have taken the abuse!

Did we kill the joy of crochet in my sister? Not really. What she did crochet-wise for the longest time was welcome new *cars* into the family with throws for the backseat or trunk that color-coordinated with the automobile's paint and upholstery. If any of her family suffered through a car's breaking down, they were going to stay warm in style. And the vehicles didn't complain about the extra weight.

Now my sister has discovered quilting and the rest, as they say, is history. Her quilts are truly works of art and the best part about it is: no gauge is required.

The Great Finishing Fake-Out

One of the things that always throws me when I am trying to figure out when a crochet project will be finished, either because I have a deadline coming up or my daughter wants to wear it to school, or even just because I am sick of it and want it to be done, darn it, is the actual finishing part. I can't tell you how many times I wind up swearing in the middle of the night because I want to finish something before I go to bed and the lightbulb goes on in my head and I realize the darn thing is taking longer to finish that it did to crochet.

More than likely the pieces have to be blocked, because a lot of crochet looks like a damp dishrag between the time you end off the last stitch and you get to actually wear or use it. Then it has to be stitched together if it was made in pieces. Sometimes I whipstitch garments or afghans together and sometimes I crochet them together—I find the crocheting finish goes faster but I often prefer the look of the sewn one.

And of course, there are ends to be woven in—sometimes lots and lots of them.

I hate, hate, hate weaving in ends. Hate it. I am compulsive about it, too, because I hate little cut endies sticking out even more than I hate weaving them in. So I am always pondering just where the best place to hide an end is. At least once a year, I threaten to design something in which the ends turn into a decorative application of some sort (fringe? bows?) just so I could get out of the "twelve hours to finish this piece" jail. Actually, my loathing of end-weaving-in is probably a major part of my felting obsession. You do have to tuck in the ends before you felt, but you don't have to be compulsive about it because the ends will felt in along with the rest of the piece.

The other thing I realize when I go into finishing mode, is how very not portable it is. Since I crochet all the time, a lot of my crocheting projects are portable. If I only got to crochet when I was home, days would go by when I didn't have a hook in my hand, and that's no good. But I can't weave in ends on a moving bus, block in the parking lot outside of dance class, or sew seams at a party while people are talking to me. Finishing requires too much attention and too many tools to be a go-anywhere stage in your project.

But ah, when the finishing is finished—what a rush. I am happy each and every time I finish crocheting something, but when it is all pressed and sewed up and I am wearing it or displaying it—wow. I feel so enormously clever. I feel like I have accomplished something. I am supercrocheter!

If only the feeling lasted longer than the finishing time . . .

The Day I Ran Out of Yarn: A Horror Story

While I am a big supporter of ideas such as the Worldwide Knit/ Crochet in Public Day, around here every day is crochet in public day. I am not as organized as those women I have heard about who have a crochet project in the car, one in the den, and one in the bedroom so they can work on whichever one is handiest, but I do tend to have two or three project bags sitting by my chair and I grab one whenever I go out the door.

But last week, the unthinkable happened. I grabbed the bag I wanted but had forgotten to "reload" the night before when I finished off a skein of yarn. Here I was, trapped, in a government office that gives out numbers like they do at the deli counter, only with *no yarn*. You can't imagine the cold chills that ran through me when I realized this. Because I didn't realize right away . . . no, the afghan block teased me. I grabbed up the square in progress, started stitching away, and after a half a dozen double crochets, what was in my left hand where the working yarn should be? Nothing.

I searched through the bag—I saw some purple in there; surely it had to be the new skein of yarn. But no. Since I already had my deli number and there was no possible hope of having it called in the next two hours, I ran outside to check the car. Surely the purple skein had dropped out of my bag and I would rescue it, have a good laugh, and get back to making afghan squares. But no. Maybe another, different project was still in the car. Even if it had been abandoned long ago, there must be a skein of yarn for something in there somewhere. No again. Sadly, I dragged myself back in to the office to face my interminable wait, crochet-less.

If time flies when you are having fun, it drags like crazy when you have nothing at all to do but watch the fifty people ahead of you transact tedious government business. "Buck up," I said to myself, "it's only a couple of hours of your life. You can get through this without having something to do with your hands." That positive attitude lasted for about five minutes and then my mind began to wander . . .

Perhaps I could unravel some of the squares I had already made, and make them again. Hmmmm . . . no, the idea of undoing all that lovely work made me cringe and the problem with afghan squares is that no matter how interesting the square pattern, odds are, you are going to be a little bored with them by the time you finish them all, so it wasn't as if I had a burning desire to make more than the thirty-six I had already signed on for. Fifteen minutes down, who knew how many to go?

Maybe I could use some of the long tails I had left on for sewing up. No, I was going to need those long tails someday soon, and the only thing more irritating than not having anything to crochet during a long wait has to be weaving in 300,000 ends. I knew! I could start sewing some of the finished squares together—that would be productive! I started digging in the bag again, but sadly only one completed square sat next to the half-finished one. Could I sew the finished half to the full square? That didn't make sense, even in my desperate state. Another twenty minutes down.

This being July, no one was wearing any sweaters or shawls with patterns I could ponder. There weren't even any handmade blankets on the numerous crying babies. I swear that the clock stopped—if I go to hell when I die, this is what it will be like. I read every word in the forms in my hand and then every article in the weekly free paper. I looked around for anything to use as yarn, wondered if I could go to jail for unraveling the American flag so I could crochet the thread, and sized up the heft of the security guard and wondered if he was armed . . .

And then they called my number. Safe! Four minutes later, I was on my way home, lamenting the loss of two good crocheting hours but knowing I was nearer the purple yarn with every passing mile. It was okay to be projectless on the way home—I don't crochet in the car when I am driving. Well, maybe during traffic jams, a little bit . . .

It's Possible I Might Sort Of Be a Yarn Snob

At least that's what my friend Remi tells me. Remi has met no yarn that she cannot see the good in—where I see cheap and scratchy, she sees inexpensive and durable. Where I see fibers not found in nature as a bad thing, she sees easy care and cleaning. Nothing repels baby spit-up like 100 percent acrylic. Where I see fun fur or sparkles and cringe, she sees bright and cheerful and fun. It isn't that she would say no to some luscious dusty rose alpaca or a big old pile of hand-painted silk; it's that she wouldn't say no to some neon orange 100 percent acrylic bargain brand, either. And I would, I definitely would.

It isn't that I don't get the upside of inexpensive acrylic yarns—they last forever, can stand up to constant use and cleaning, come in every color in the rainbow (and several that Mother Nature I am sure never intended), and an afghan's worth of them will not require six months of credit card payments. They are readily available in all parts of the country and can be used in all sorts of projects from afghans to baby clothes. Intellectually, I understand. Tactilely, I am just not sold.

I want to feel natural fibers running through my fingers as I work. I want to pet the alpaca at the fiber farm, and then buy the fleece or the yarn that came from his furry butt. I want organic cottons that will weather like my favorite pair of ancient jeans or linens that are sharp and crisp and then soften with use. I want colors that glow with inner warmth and call to mind beautiful sunsets or roiling ocean waves. In short, I want the expensive stuff.

How expensive? I think the most I ever spent on a skein of yarn was sixty-nine dollars for some gorgeous teal qiviut. Sadly, there was not much teal qiviut about 213 yards of a fine-gauge yarn. It hasn't turned into anything yet—it's still in a skein, looking lovely. And that might be all it has to do to make me happy—I haven't decided yet. Am I happy with my purchase despite the fact that it took me three days of petting it to get up the nerve to plunk down the cold hard cash? Even if it never turns into a scarf? Even if there are starving crocheters in wherever that would never in their lives buy yarn made from the undercoat of a musk ox? Yes. And hey, maybe I could write it off on my taxes, since I just wrote about it!

To rationalize my yarn purchases, I have gone from saying, "This yarn is X dollars per skein" to "This sweater will cost X dollars." I find per project costs to make much more sense to my occasionally cheapo brain than a per-skein price. And with some yarns, if you figure out how much they cost per ounce you realize that you could have bought filet mignon or raw gold more cost effectively. But even the cheapo part of my brain doesn't object to paying a few bucks for a high-quality item that I know I am going to get a lot of use out of . . . even if I have to wash it by hand.

Does this make me a yarn snob? Remi says yes (but she smiles when she says it, so it's okay). I say no—I am not a yarn snob so much as an experienced fiber artist who knows how to purchase the supplies that make me happiest. *Snob* has such a negative connotation. Perhaps I could be a natural fiber enthusiast instead.

Crocheter vs. Stash

The dream: Okay, I am going to clean out the stash today. I am going to organize, sort, make notes so I don't buy the same thing twice, and dig out all of the things I won't get to in this lifetime and get rid of them. I am going to finish all the works-in-progress, or at least put the patterns and parts together in an organized fashion if it turns out there are rather a few more of them than I remember. I will condense, I will combine, I will find room in the stash closet where none existed before and this time, *this* time, I will not fill up the newly created space with random yarn purchases (which are not my fault because as we all know, nature abhors a vacuum and you can't fight physics). I will once and for all put all of my unassigned hooks in one needle case so that I will have at my fingertips the one that I want when I need it, which will save me tons of money because I won't have to run to the store for hooks every time I start a new project, and therefore will spend less time succumbing to temptation in the form of wool. And I will do it all today. Amen.

The reality: I decide the first order of business will be to get all the stash in one place. It's all in the stash closet, right? Oh, except for the underbed storage containers in the guest room. And the pile of wool in the cedar chest. Um, there might be a bag (or six) in the living room—stuff I thought I would start on right away so it wasn't worth stuffing it into the closet. And the bag in the car that I am trying to pretend I didn't buy ... and if it's not in the house, it's not in the stash, right? Oh, and the leftovers from design jobs that I don't think I can part with yet—at least not until the patterns are published because who knows what might happen during the photo shoots. If I had to remake something, I would need the same dye lot. Since that yarn is stored with the work yarn, it doesn't really count as stash yarn. However, I should probably put all the yarn together because now every single thing will be organized, so I decide I need that, too. This part might take a little longer than I thought. And maybe I need more space ... like perhaps a spare house. Okay, moving on.

I am going to empty out all the containers and sort everything by weight—sock yarns with sock yarns up to bulky with bulky. Darn, I have a whoooooooole lot of sock yarn. Well, does the light worsted go with DK or with worsted weight? Is that organic cotton a bulky or a worsted? What the heck weight is baby yarn, anyway? Where did all this stuff come from? Maybe I should sort by color. I need to lie down, but there isn't any room because there is a two-foot-deep layer of yarn on the bed. I think I will have a snack instead.

Postsnack, I decide that before I sort anything, I should get rid of all the skeins and partials that I don't want. If I give some things to the local senior center, they will be very grateful and I will have less bulk to organize. This is a fine idea. So I will now look at every skein of yarn and make a decision as to whether it's something I really think I will use. While I am at it, I will examine all the WIPS. If I decide not to bother with something, I will rip it out instead of keeping it in its partial state, and if it's ripped out it's yarn, not a WIP so should be counted with the yarn. Maybe I should bring out the ball winder so I can rip out more efficiently ... hmmmm ...

Four and a half hours later, I still haven't laid hands and eyeballs on every skein and WIP, and it's getting to be pretty near the time that I need to be finished so I can go pick up the kiddo from school and take her to dance class. Maybe I should start putting stuff away—the pile has to be lower now, right, after all my rigorous pondering? I look over to the garbage bag where I put the yarn to be donated. It isn't very full—in fact, it only has five sad partial skeins and some baby yarn (because this way I don't have to decide what weight that is). I should maybe think a little harder about giving more away, but decide I don't have any more pondering time available to me right now. I put the garbage bag in the back of the car. And stop for a late lunch. And some crocheting—if I get going on some of these WIPs, I would surely make progress in the decluttering department.

Having thoroughly lost track of time, I now run to pick up my daughter, walk the dog, and run to dance class. Then we have to eat, then I have to nag about homework, and then I hear I am supposed to have made two trays of brownies for school tomorrow. So I make some brownies. And the kiddo goes to bed.

Now it's 10:00 P.M. I am fried and have, conservatively speaking, ten thousand bits of yarn lying around. Sorting be darned, I am going to just shove all this stuff back in the boxes and into the closet and will get it really, really organized tomorrow. Although oddly, the amount of yarn that came out of the boxes doesn't seem to want to go back into the boxes. I believe that exposure to light and air has made the stash expand.

Just past midnight, I decide that if I have to go through it all again tomorrow anyway, it might be just as easy to dump the remaining skeins onto the floor. In fact, I could sleep under some of them and turn the heat down a bit—yarn makes great insulation—and that would be really energy conscious. So this is what I do. The only problem is the panic attack I have at 3:00 A.M. when I get up to use the bathroom, step on a skein of mohair and scream, thinking I have just crushed the dog. I wake up just enough to realize that since the mohair didn't bark it wasn't the dog, and if it was anything else living I really don't want to know about it right now, so I move on and go back to bed.

In the morning the alarm goes off, and in the stark light of day I see my room—it looks as if a small bomb exploded in the middle of a yarn store managed by someone with eclectic tastes. My daughter wanders in, rubbing her eyes, and demands to know why she has to clean her room if mine gets to look like this. And why is it so cold? I put my head under the pillow, count to ten, and then get moving to face the day.

After I deliver my daughter, ever the critic, to school, I decide I have to deal with the stash explosion, and sooner rather than later. Sorting be darned, I squish and squeeze until every last skein of it that came out of the closet fits back in the closet. Instead of the delight of a job well done, I have sort of a sickly feeling that I just wasted two full days getting nothing done that should have been spent writing or designing or doing some other income-producing work.

I vow never to clean out the stash again. Some things just shouldn't be messed with.

Too Much Yarn

Just the other day I uttered a phrase that stopped traffic in my household, a phrase I never in a million years thought I would utter. I was sorting through yet another box of yarn that appeared as if by magic, trying to lower the square footage of wool that is all over my living room, and in frustration I yelled out, "I have too much yarn!" You could hear crickets chirping in the aftermath—my daughter looked at me as if I had three heads; even the dog cocked her head and started to slink slowly away from the crazy woman. Did I really say I had too much yarn? Was I sick with a fever?

I think most crocheters have a personal set point at which the stash becomes "too much yarn." For some crocheters, a dozen or so skeins are too much. Others cut back on purchases when they run out of room in a predetermined space—a storage bin, spare closet, the guest room. I have been crocheting for more years than several of you reading this have been alive, yet I had never before hit my own "too much yarn" point. And there is yarn everywhere. I am not the most organized person in the world on my best day, and I have a pretty high tolerance for yarn stacked in common living spaces, yet I have finally cracked. There is too much yarn in my house.

I have always been acquisitive as far as yarn goes. I remember walking to the local five-and-ten store when I was in grade school, pondering all the colors available in one-ounce skeins, and taking my time choosing which one or two to spend my meager funds on. When a local discount store went out of business, I went back day after day as the close-out discount got larger and scooped up skeins (the big ones! Four whole ounces!) for loose change. I made granny square after granny square with a different color combination in each one. In high school, I bought large bags of tangled skeins of acrylic for next to nothing from a yarn shop in the mall and spent hours and hours detangling them and winding them into balls. Then? More granny squares!

College brought a move to the big city (NYC, if you are keeping score) and exposure to my first real local yarn store (LYS). It specialized in the products of a certain European manufacturer and I thought I had died and gone to yarn heaven. The colors, the textures, the natural fibers—yum to all of it. When school became too stressful, I spent time there petting skeins and paging through pattern books. I do not want to talk about what percentage of my student loan checks went to yarn and needles, but I did make all my Christmas gifts during those years so I rationalized that it all worked out in the end, budget-wise. I alternated the pricier trips to the LYS with some bargain hunting at the discount store down Sixth Avenue—*one project in Phildar, one in Lion Brand, repeat from * around.

After school I hit the road and my yarn came with me. I traveled, first the United States and then the world, caring for the costumes of various and sundry dance companies. I shopped in yarn stores all over, which was great so far as variety goes, not so hot if I underestimated the yardage for a project and had to try to match a dye lot. I recall phoning a store in New Jersey when I was in Colorado and having the yarn I needed shipped to Arizona. When I filled out the paperwork to get my road trunks through customs when we traveled abroad, I was always careful to list a "canvas bag with yarn and crochet hooks," which was specific enough verbiage to get us through the red tape but vague enough that it covered whatever project I was working on at the time. I remember many of my travels through the projects made from the yarn I brought home. I still have vivid memories of the little shop where I found some green and tan DK weight off the beaten path on the North Island of New Zealand—every time I see the sweater, I remember that trip.

None of this led to a huge stash, however. I bought yarn all the time, but I made it up pretty soon thereafter. I remember knitting the sleeves of that green and tan sweater in San Diego, which was my next stop after Wellington. I bought yarn, I crocheted it up, I left a trail of finished objects behind me as gifts, or it moved into my suitcase in the form of clothing rather than crafts projects.

So I guess my serious stash habits began with the purchase of my first house. I saw some yarn or some patterns on sale, and I bought them. If I wasn't going to work on something right away, I would box it up and put it in the attic. I had a pretty good handle on what projects were lined up in what box and even kept the patterns and the yarn together so I wasn't buying yarn with no purpose in mind. We moved, and the stash moved with us. It was still pretty well contained, although it had to move from the attic to the guest room closet in the interest of keeping the fiber in the proper environment, heat- and humidity-wise.

And in the new environment, it started to spread. It outgrew the closet expanded into an underbed storage box or two (or four) and into the cedar chest. And of course the projects I was going to work on "soon" migrated into the living room—there was no point in packing that stuff away if I was going to need it in the very near future. And there wasn't any room anywhere else, anyway. As I discovered new and different fibers, I bought more yarn. When I found a great sale, I bought more yarn. Then I discovered sheep and wool festivals and I bought *a lot* more yarn. I started spinning and bought roving, which turned into . . . You guessed it. More yarn. Still, I didn't think I had too much. And then I changed careers.

A few years back I started designing crochet patterns professionally. If you ever talk to crochet designers and ask about entering the field, we will all tell you the same thing—it pays crap and you could make more money per hour working at a fast-food joint. "Don't do it," we cry, "you will be sucked in and never get out!" So then why do we do it? The glory of seeing our name in print? The burning desire to share our artistic vision with the world at large? Nah, it's the little voice in the back of our head that tells us that if we work as a designer we get free yarn. And who can resist free yarn? I can't. And therein lies the rub.

It started out with a very few companies offering me a little bit of yarn to swatch. Yarn companies like it when designers use their yarns, as it increases demand for their products. But they can't just hand out a bunch of yarn to everyone who asks, so my freebies were pretty much bits and bobs of new things and leftovers from design jobs I had actually sold. As my name got out in the industry, my work started to be seen in books and magazines, and I attended more and more trade shows, more companies were willing to give me a skein or two here and there. I loved them, petted them, swatched them (or didn't, right away—we were rapidly approaching the way-more-yarn-than-time conundrum), and put them with the other yarns in my stash.

Soon, yarn started arriving in big boxes—not just yarn for swatching, but for the various designs I had sold. You always ask for the amount of yarn you think you need, then a little bit more just in case you need it. No one wants to have to do that interstate (or depending on where the warehouse is, international) dye-lot chase. Often the shipper will throw in a little extra, too—they get the worst end of the dye-lot chase if it happens, so they *really* want to make sure you have enough yarn. Because of this, you have leftovers too nice to throw away, but you are probably sick of the color by the time the project is over with, so it goes in the stash closet to mellow for a while until you think of a use for it. As I went from working on one or two designs at a time to six or seven or twelve designs at a time, the yarn deliveries increased. But I was still fine—I had a nice stash and it was getting nicer all the time. So what if sleepover guests couldn't hang any clothes in the closet? Isn't that what their suitcase was for?

And then it happened. I agreed to design a book of afghans. I thought choosing the colors and estimating the yardage was the hard part . . . and then the boxes began to arrive. Over three hundred skeins of yarn in a three-week period—and that was on top of my regular, everyday stash that was several hundred skeins all on its own. Yarn was everywhere. Even when I sent some of it out to friends to make the models for me, the pieces and leftovers came back. I went from stalking the UPS driver to praying he wasn't stopping at my house whenever I saw the big brown truck come up the block. A neighbor went on a catalog shopping spree and I nearly had a heart attack for a week when her deliveries came by!

What do you do with too much yarn? My daughter would happily take it, but she is even less organized than I am if you can imagine such a thing, and that doesn't really get it out of my house. It simply moves the clutter from one room to another. So I engaged on a campaign to lower the yarn density of my house.

Plan one: Pawn it off on a friend who does not have quite my stash problem. I set up a day and invited my buddy to go "shopping in the dining room." She was delighted with all the goodies, and I believe caught a wicked case of startitis, which I feel sort of bad about, but not bad enough that I wouldn't do it again.

Plan two: Find someone who would be happy to take the odd balls and partial skeins. I implemented this plan by adopting a local senior citizen's crochet and knit group that makes blankets for shelters of both the human and animal variety. They can incorporate single skeins into works of art and my donations mean they can produce more while spending less of their own money. And there have been no records of cats complaining about the color choices in their blankets.

Plan three: Get real about what will and will not conceivably be wanted in the future and increase the amount of yarn that goes to plan one and plan two. It doesn't matter how much I give away, more always arrives, so keeping the pipeline flowing might avoid another meltdown on my part.

Plan four: Buy high-rise beds for all of the residents of the house, including the dog. It might be harder to get in and out of bed at night for all concerned, but imagine how much larger I could make the underbed storage crates. Meaning more stash for me! Hey, I want to declutter a bit, not go cold turkey and stashless. That's just crazy talk.

The Secret Life of a Crochet Designer

It all starts in the ether—somebody, somewhere has a glimmer of an idea. It may be inspired by a yarn or a stitch, by the stars and the moon, a breakfast cereal, or anything else. But somebody somewhere has an idea for a crochet design.

1. To sell a crochet design to a publisher of some sort, you need a swatch, a sketch, and probably a schematic. You swatch, you sketch, you rip out, you erase. Lather, rinse, and repeat as necessary until you get all of those three things to look like you want them to—a crocheted fabric you are happy with, a sketch of what the final garment will look like, and a schematic of what the pieces are and their general shape. You whomp all this stuff together with a designer bio (that says how wonderful you are) and a paragraph or two about your genius design and why it needs to be shared with the world, and you decide to send it off to an editor.

2. You download the designer guidelines, look at the calendar, and realize that you have swatched something that would keep an Eskimo warm ... and the editor of your dream publication is currently reviewing summer. Darn. You can submit it anyway and hope it doesn't get lost, put it in your file cabinet until the appropriate time (and hope it doesn't get lost), or decide to publish it yourself. In the meantime you had better swatch something summery, don't you think? If you decide to self-publish, skip to number 8.

3. It's time and you mail off or e-mail your submission packet. You know it will take six to eight weeks at best to hear back from someone, but this does not stop you from obsessively checking your e-mail, starting about twenty minutes after you think the packet has been received. Surely your piece is just so darn wonderful that the editor will have to accept it within seconds of its crossing his or her desk, lest your genius get away. This does not happen.

4. Wait and wait and wait and wait. Six weeks go by, then eight, now you are frantic. You know that pestering the assistants at the magazine is unlikely to make you any friends, yet you consider calling. You go online and ask everyone you ever knew who ever submitted a design for consideration anywhere if he or she has heard anything about this particular issue/deadline. No one knows anything more than you do.

5a. Sometimes, you get a "thanks, but no thanks" letter. Rejected—boooooooooo . . . Sometimes you don't hear anything at all, but find out via your trusty Internet sleuthing that those whose designs were chosen have already gotten contracts and gotten started so you know this wasn't your time. You might now decide to self-publish; if you do, skip to number 8. You might also decide to submit somewhere else (although you now have missed the seasonal deadline) or rework the piece before shipping it off again. Or,

5b. Your design was accepted—yaaaaay! And then quickly boo when you realize how much you have to get done and how little time you have to do it. You get a contract in the mail, some of which makes as much sense to you as a foreign language in which you are not fluent. You ask your cousin the real estate attorney for help. He laughs and says it doesn't make any sense to him, either. You do as much due diligence as you can and then sign it and send it in—you are so happy to get published, it isn't as if you are going to say no, is it?

6. Now you have to tell the publisher's office how much yarn you need so they can get it shipped to you, and by the way did they mention they need the sample crocheted and the pattern written in 1,200 sizes about forty-five minutes after the yarn is expected to get to you? That's not a problem, is it? No, of course it isn't—all will be well.

7. You have to get the model made now, either by doing it yourself or hiring a contractor. So you stalk the UPS man, waiting for your yarn to come in so you can get started. As soon as the sample is finished, you fly to the delivery service of your choice and ship the model off. Amen. The pattern gets e-mailed and passed along to the tech editor. It will be a few months before your pattern hits the newsstands, so you are free for a while—maybe to get started on something else. Skip off to number 9.

8. The joys of self-publishing. You have to do (or pay someone else to do) all the things that a big publisher would do. However, the upside is that you should get a larger share of the profit from the pattern sales, should there actually be any sales. You don't get to call someone to order yarn—you pretty much have to go buy some. You still need to get the sample crocheted and the pattern written in 1,200 sizes, but you can be a little flexible about the deadline—hey, you're the publisher.

So you make the model, take the photos, write the pattern, send the pattern out for technical editing or test crocheting or both, devise a layout, investigate internet pay-per-download delivery systems, and check out printing hard copies to sell either at wholesale or retail. Then you, too, skip off to number 9.

9. The tech editor has a question, or two or three. You go over whatever he or she has "clarified" in your instructions, but they aren't any more clear to you so you ponder and reread until it all makes sense. Often you find that the technical edit did in fact make things better in the long run, so you are happy. At least you hope things are better, because you wrote the darn pattern so long ago now that you aren't completely sure what it was that you did.

10a. If you are being published by someone else, the magazine or book finally hits the public eye. You are very excited to see your name in print, and in such good company. There are some really great things in there along with yours! You drag the magazine around to show everyone you know, even the ones who don't crochet. Some are more impressed than others, but all of your friends are excited for you. You feel like a big dork but you might even get a copy framed—it is a big deal. Or,

10b. You publish your design online and it finally hits the public eye. You are very excited to see your name in print and in such good company. There are some really great things out there in indie publishing world! You drag the pattern around to show everyone you know, even the ones who don't crochet. Some are more impressed than others, but all of your friends are excited for you. You feel like a big dork but you might even get a copy framed—it is a big deal.

11a. You wait for the check to come in. You wait and you wait, and you stalk the mailman the way you stalked the UPS guy for the yarn. Eventually it comes and you are very happy—you actually made money from your passion for crochet. Of course, by the time you figure out how many hours you spent, both in preparation for selling the design and in getting it all done, you realize that you could have made way more money flipping burgers. But what the hell, you are now a professional designer. Cash the check, take your family and friends (provided you don't have too many of either) out for a decent lunch, and start all over again. Or,

11b. You wait for the orders, and therefore some money, to come in. You wait and you wait and you check your PayPal account constantly. Eventually some orders come in and you are very happy—you actually made money from your passion for crochet. Of course by the time you figure out how many hours you spent, both in preparation for selling the design and in getting it all done, you realize that you could have made way more money flipping burgers. But what the hell, you are now a professional designer. Cash the check, take your family and friends (provided you don't have too many of either) out for a decent lunch, and start all over again.

If you are serious about working as a crochet designer full-time, the minute you submit that first swatch, you submit six more, and then start planning the next six. You seed the clouds of publications by spreading submissions far and wide, because if you don't get a bunch sold, then you are not going to make enough money to buy cat food, let alone pay any of the big bills. The same goes for independent publishing—one down, a bunch more to go, to get some cash flow. Plus, you keep submitting to the magazines anyway because if you get a pattern in one of the bigger ones every now and again, it's good publicity—it gets your name out there.

Now instead of one pattern in development, you have a bunch—yarn is piling up in your living room; you are begging people you know to work as model makers, or even models; and you just pray you get the right yarn matched up with the right pattern as sample garments come and go.

You're probably still not as rich as Croesus, but you're having a great time. People warned you that getting into publishing would take all the fun out of crocheting, that it would then be a chore rather than something you do for fun, but it's all fun. The first time you see someone out there in the real world, wearing something she made from one of your designs, is an unbelievable feeling—all the aggravation was worth it.

When aspiring designers ask about getting into the business, they are often told not to bother. It's a lot of work, often for little remuneration, and you will work 24/7 to get established. And that really is true. But have you noticed that there are a whole lot of crochet designers out there? That's because when the designs come to you, they demand to be set free—best not to stand in their way.

Passing On the Yarn Gene

Simply by being a child of mine, my daughter spends a fair amount of time surrounded by yarn. It's here in the house (as in everywhere in the house), turns up in the car, and I am rarely without a project stuffed in a tote bag when we are out and about. But she always had a take-it-or-leave-it attitude with yarny crafts—yarn was fine, but other things were equally fine.

I started dragging her to sheep and wool festivals because I wanted to go to them. I didn't have much arm-twisting to do after the first one because there were animals to pet, and she has always loved animals. Then she was drawn to the colors and textures of the different yarns and she always, always wanted to try every craft she saw. Which is why we have a *kumihimo* braider, a spinning wheel, a rigid heddle loom, and a box of acid dye colors stuffed in the various niches in my home that are not already full of yarn. I just knew that something, sometime, would awaken the yarny goddess within her. But no luck.

I taught her to knit; she could take it or leave it. Ditto the crocheting, the braiding, the spinning, the weaving (the soap making, the scrapbooking—you get the idea). It isn't that she couldn't do any of these crafts on her own. Her desire to do any one craft long enough to get fast at it just wasn't strong enough. And I always wondered if she would turn sort of anticrafty so as to establish her own hobby identity as separate from mine.

I tried to encourage her but only a little bit, so I wouldn't turn into the yarny equivalent of a stage mother. As she got a little older she would point out patterns in the books or magazines or pull a particular favorite yarn out of my stash and ask me to make her a garment to wear to school.

"You could do that yourself," I pointed out.

"Yes, but you are faster," she replied.

"You would get faster if you practiced more."

(*long dramatic sigh*)

And then I would make her the garment anyway. I love making things for her, and as the teenage years approach like an oncoming freight train, some part of me treasures the fact that she will still be seen in public in something that came from my own two hands.

One day at Mecca (the Sheep and Wool Festival in Rhinebeck, New York, for those of you who are misguided enough to think that yarn heaven is elsewhere), we were tooling around the booth of a wonderfully talented dyer and choosing roving to go with our just-purchased drop spindles. A gray-haired woman with an armload of color looked at me and shook her head with a slight smile on her face. "You know you are taking a real chance bringing her in here," she said. I must have looked puzzled, because my daughter has always had excellent shop manners (she definitely got the shopping gene from me), and I thought the woman was implying that children shouldn't be shopping in this setting. Then she smiled more broadly and said, "You are setting that poor child on the path to a lifelong fiber addiction!" "Well," I said with a laugh, "it's too late for me; she might as well come along for the ride." Everyone nearby smiled and we bought our roving and moved on.

It was easy for me to laugh. I already knew about my own fiber addiction and the kid had always been more interested in the shopping than the crafting. I am sure if I had some other type of lifestyle, I mean hobby, and if there were weekend-long festivals with cool things to buy, she would have been equally interested (or not interested, as the case may be). Plus being little and cute has its advantages. Some wonderful vendors at Mecca gave her gifts of fiber and tools because she was polite and interested—and free stuff is almost better than shopping. I guess in the back of my mind I figured the fiber gene had skipped a generation—she was interested enough because it surrounds her, but the attraction to the needle arts was not rampant on a molecular level.

But this summer, everything changed. We were at yet another yarn and fiber event, and in the interest of having something to do while I schmoozed (or more likely, because she heard that the attendees of this particular class, Crochet for Kids, were getting a really awesome goody bag), she took a crochet class. The instructor was great (and not me, a definite advantage), her friend was sitting next to her (and has a preexisting interest in crochet), the goody bag was in fact awesome and full of yarn sure to warm the cockles of an almost-twelve-year-old heart (it was brightly colored! And fuzzy! And sparkly! And all three at once!!!), and she learned how to make a really fast project (instant gratification). She had a great time and was smiling ear to ear when I collected her from class.

She crocheted all that afternoon and into the evening, presenting some of her friends with her very first handmade flowers. She crocheted in the car on the way home during a fairly long drive. She crocheted after we got home—making flowers for her friends and bags for every electronic item she ever owned (a not inconsiderable number). She pulled out the stash she had been given over the years, unearthed a wicker basket in which to store it, and started poring over crochet books. The next time we had to go out on an errand that we knew would involve some tedious waiting time, I reached out for my tote bag full of yarn and saw that she already had hers on her arm. The fiber gene, hiding all this time, had kicked in with a vengeance. My child was hooked!

And I was delighted. Does that make me a bad mother?

Part Three

Goth Princess Toilet Paper Doll

Well, if we are going to make toilet paper covers shaped

like women, let's at least advance to this century, no?

I had more fun putting this together than I ever

did making a Southern belle! Let your (subversive

crocheter's) mind run free and accessorize your Goth

princess as you see fit.

Materials:

- About 150 yards worsted-weight (CYCA 4, medium) 100% acrylic in black or another tragic, dark colorway. The model shown used half a skein of Caron Simply Soft in Black, color #9727.
- Crochet hook size H/8/5 mm, or size needed to get gauge
- Roll of toilet paper
- Bargain-brand 11- to 12-inch "fashion doll"—the cheaper, the better as you are going to abuse it!
- Permanent-bond glue for attaching pieces to the doll
- Assorted crafts supplies for accessories. Go wild, but I used: white glue to stiffen the Mohawk, purple paint for hair, leather or faux leather scraps for the bodice and cuff, small silver-colored flat beads for studs, tiny silver jewelry findings for earrings, 12 to 18 inches of silver chain, a fine-point permanent black marker for lipstick (and I wish my hands were steady enough that I could have done a tattoo!), and some replica beer bottles I found in the miniatures department of a local crafts store.

Gauge: 12 sts and 9 rows = 4 inches in dc

The Skirt (TP Cover):

Ch 48. Join into a ring with sl st to 1st ch, being careful not to twist the ch. Ch 3.

Rnd 1: Dc in each ch around, join with sl st to beg ch. Ch 3. (48 dc)

Rnd 2: Skip 1st dc, dc in each dc around, join with sl st to beg ch. Ch 3.

Rep rnd 2 until work measures 4 3/4 inches long, or long enough to comfortably cover the height of your chosen roll of toilet paper. Begin your decreases:

Dec rnd 1: Sk 1st dc, dc in each of next 5 dc, dc2tog, *dc in each of next 6 dc, dc2tog. Repeat from * around, join with sl st to beg ch. (42 dc)

Dec rnd 2: Sk 1st dc, dc in each of next 4 dc, dc2tog, *dc in each of next 5 dc, dc2tog. Repeat from * around, join with sl st to beg ch. (36 dc)

Dec rnds 3–6: Continue in pattern as established, working one less dc between decreases for each row. End off. (12 dc after rnd 6)

Assembly:

If you are going to give the doll a mad hairstyle, it is easier to do that before assembly. I saturated the doll's hair with white glue, fastened it above her head with a rubber band, and allowed it to dry overnight. Then I chopped off the ends to produce a modified Mohawk, and added the purple paint.

Put the skirt over the toilet paper roll, insert the doll through the top opening, and push her feet all the way down until they touch the bottom of the roll. Thread the yarn tail through the last row and pull it tight around her waist, then glue it into place.

Cut the leather scrap into a rectangle and glue it down for a bodice—no worries if it's crooked or ill-fiting; it will fit the style of our tp girl! Then go to town with decorations—earrings, chains, safety pins, black lipstick and nails—whatever suits your fancy.

Display with pride!

Crocheters, the Silent Majority

Although you may have heard the urban legend than crocheters outnumber knitters three to one, there isn't much hard scientific data to back that up. Research does exist on crafter demographics in America, but there is a bit of a muddle between who is a crocheter and who is a knitter, and of course many of us are both. Don't get me wrong—no one doubts that there are more crocheters than knitters; it's just the order of magnitude by which we rule that is in question.

Which makes it a little strange to me that certain yarn stores are often not equal-opportunity places to buy fiber, but specifically knitting stores. I had heard about this discrimination, and honestly questioned it a bit, but then I stopped in a few new-to-me LYSs and got a sample of what some of my sisters with hooks were talking about.

I guess I don't identify myself as a crocheter when I enter a new store, or as a knitter, either, for that matter. I just tend to wander in and pet what I like, and I have never had anyone question my right to be there. But after hearing some horror stories about crochet-phobes in yarn shops, I tried an experiment. In one particularly well-known big-city store, the crochet books, most of which were several years old, were placed in a dusty rack by the ladies' room. There were about three crochet hooks, buried at toddler-eye level under umpteen thousand styles of knitting needles. When I asked where the crochet items were, the store owner looked at me with a bemused expression, as if she was waiting for me to say I was just kidding or something. When I didn't, she pretty much lost interest in waiting on me at all. Needless to say, I didn't buy anything at that store, and I started to see that maybe my crocheting friends who cried discrimination had a valid point.

But guys, we outnumber the knitters. We really do. And there is strength in numbers. We just need to get a little organized about how to wield our power.

For one thing, we should not support shops that do not value our custom. Which isn't to say we should be nasty, because that rarely gets anyone anywhere, but if you walk into a store and are treated rudely, walk right back out. Even if you will then have to make a trip somewhere else to get what you need. Make sure you tell them why you are leaving or your leaving doesn't help change their behavior! If you are too shy (or shocked by the snark) to say something directly, drop the person's superior a quick note or an e-mail after you get home. Something like:

> Dear Store Owner:
>
> When I went into your shop today and asked about crochet items, I was sneered at by one of your employees who told me there was nothing there for me. I know it wasn't you because no store owner would be crazy enough

to turn away money in this or any economy.

I am bringing this to your attention because I feel certain that as a savvy business owner you would want all potential customers to be made welcome, and if I don't share my experience with you, you won't have the opportunity to fix it. So I will be back in your store in a month or so to give you a chance to rectify the bad impression you made. Shame on you if you make the same mistake twice, because neither I nor any of my crocheting friends will give you the opportunity to do it a third time.

Sincerely,
A Crocheter

The flip side of this is to make sure, when you see a growing selection of crochet items in your local store or someone goes out of their way to help you, that you leave a little of your hard-earned cash behind—and again tell them why.

Dear Store Owner:

So many independent yarn shops are not crochet-friendly that I wanted to tell you I was delighted by the excellent service I received today. I am happy to note that you are now carrying the newest crochet magazines. I want to let you know that I will buy the ones I don't subscribe to already from you instead of the ginormous chain store, because I know my purchases make a difference.

See you soon,
A Crocheter

And then do it—support the shops that support your craft.

Complaining to one another is not going to change the ways of the fiber world but getting out there and making ourselves more visible might. If there aren't any crochet lessons where you live, teach some. Wear your crochet with pride, and if someone confuses it with knitting, explain politely that it's crocheted and what the difference is. If someone presumes that you only crochet because you haven't learned to knit yet, tell that person that crocheting is your needlecraft of choice and you are quite happy with it—you crochet out of love for the form, not lack of knowledge or skill. Rioting is not the answer (although wouldn't it be fun? A crochet riot? I can't imagine!), but speaking up is. There are so many of us that eventually, people will have to listen.

Ten Things Crocheters Would Like to Say to the Rest of the World, but Most Times Are Far Too Polite To

1. *"Oh, you can't crochet with that."* Yes, in fact I *can* crochet with that. If it's long and stringy, I can crochet with it. Hell, if I was desperate enough, spaghetti squash would look like a good substitute for yarn. Please stop telling me that yarn is only to knit with; it isn't. Although there are certain yarns I wouldn't want to crochet with, that's not because I can't but because I choose not to.

2. *"I thought only grandmothers crochet."* Anyone can crochet—there is no minimum age requirement. I hope I am still crocheting when I am a grandmother. But last I heard, you don't get assigned a hook and some yarn the minute one of your children gives birth (although it would be cool if we did!). There is no correlation between crochet and procreation. Unless, perhaps, you crochet sexy lingerie, but that is a whole different conversation.

3. *"Oh, you are crocheting . . . do you want to learn to knit?"* I do knit, but it is not a higher life form or something for a crocheter to aspire to. It's a different form of working with fiber. Neither is inherently better or worse; they are just different. But implying to me that I am too stupid to knit is eventually going to get me to do a little more than imply that you were too stupid to internalize the good manners I am sure your mother thought she taught you.

4. *"Oh my goodness, I would never have time to do something like that."* I do not have more than the requisite twenty-four hours in my day, either, I just choose to do a little bit more with them. I won't take shots at your sitcom habit, and you can stop assuming that my house is a mess and my dog unfed because I like to crochet in my free time. Well, my house is a mess, but I am pretty sure that even if I didn't crochet, it would still be messy. And if I don't feed the dog, she sits on the yarn until I do.

5. *"You are crocheting for charity? Wouldn't it be better to write a check?"* In the words of the Beatles, money can't buy me love. I do not give my work to others because I think it is subpar. I crochet for others whom I think need the tactile comfort a crocheted item can bring. You can't cuddle twenty-five dollars, sleep under it, or wrap it around you and know that even if times are a bit bleak right now, someone, somewhere, wanted you to know that you were not alone. There are certainly times when a charitable donation is better made as cash, but I am not going to stop crocheting blankets for Project Linus any time soon, either. I put the best of my talents to use when I crochet for others—I am not giving it away because it's awful, I am giving it away because I think it's the right thing to do.

6. "*What are you knitting?*" I am not knitting; I am crocheting. And I truly don't mind if you don't know the difference—I may not know much about your obsessive hobbies, either. But when I say it's crocheting, please don't tell me, "Same thing." They're not. Separate but equal, but not the same. And if you don't want to know anything at all about it, why did you ask what I was knitting in the first place?

7. "*You can buy that dishcloth/baby blanket/scarf-and-hat set at Wal-Mart. Why would you waste time and money making it?*" I could buy *a* hat at Wal-Mart but I can't buy *this* hat at Wal-Mart. This hat is exactly the color, shape, fiber content, and style that I want. It is unique because it is handmade. And not only will I have a good time wearing it or giving it away, but I also had a great time making it. The one at Wal-Mart might be a bit cheaper but cheap isn't always the most important thing.

8. "*That's way too expensive*" in response to a crocheted item offered for sale at a market. May I direct you to a nearby Wal-Mart? Several people have told me just today that you can get really cheap dishcloths/baby blankets/scarf-and-hat sets there.

9. "*You can't make cables/fitted garments/socks with crochet.*" Maybe you can't, but I certainly can. Want to see?

10. "*Wow, that's really cool!*" Want to learn? I can teach you—come sit here by me. Mwa ha ha ha ha ha . . .

Crochet Needs a Good PR Agency

There are those people, even in the yarn industry, who look down on crochet—they say crocheters are cheap; don't read, make ugly home decor items and boxy, ill-fitting garments, all of which are made out of granny squares; and are trapped in the outdated past. Some of these thoughts are stereotypes, maybe with a very slight basis in reality, and some are just horse puckie. In thinking about things, I realized that crochet doesn't need to change what it is to get more respect, but that we as its practitioners merely need to put a better spin on things. We don't need anything but some good PR. Herewith, my answers to the naysayers—feel free to adapt them for your own personal use.

Crocheters are cheap. You say cheap—I say thrifty. And when did thrift become a sin instead of a virtue? If your project is going to require, conservatively, thirty million yards of yarn, does it make sense to spend a dollar a yard? No matter what your income, no one in the world is going to feel comfortable lying on the couch with the dog and a small leaky child or two cuddled under an afghan whose material cost would feed a family of four for a month, including dinner out once a week. And comfort is key— we crocheters want to wrap up the world in our crocheted hugs, one person at a time. We don't want to be upset when something is used hard. We prefer to feel jubilation that we chose just the right combination of beauty and utility. Hardworking crochet needs hardworking yarn, and lots of it.

And for the odd project that requires less than a million yards, we will happily hit the LYS. It isn't that we have an aversion to pricier yarns, but that we merely like to go yarn shopping without having to arrange for a second mortgage ahead of time. Cheap? Nah, smart shoppers.

Crocheters make ugly things. Although crocheters might make certain styles of ugly things more than other crafters (I have to own up to the toilet paper covers and the bed dolls right now and get it over with—sorry, if you love them, but neither are objects of high style no matter how beautifully executed), we certainly don't have the corner on the shameful craft project market. You want to mock the '70s? Anyone remember macramé plant hangers that dripped from every ceiling? Or how the people who made a hobby out of burning brightly colored candles in chianti bottles until they had a wax sculpture that took up half the living room? Let's talk about woodburning as home decor rather than a Scouting project. Ugly craft projects abound—and they aren't all crocheted.

Crocheters don't read. Seriously, there are books on knitting history, books of knitting humor, books on the knitting lifestyle, and books and books and books of knitting patterns. What do we have? Um, this book you're reading and about a thousand leaflets. It isn't that I won't read about crocheting; it's that there haven't been all that many books available to me that piqued my interest. It's the conundrum of craft publishing. Are there no crochet books because they don't sell, or do crochet books not sell because there aren't enough good-quality ones published? And please don't show me the alleged bicraftual books that advertise themselves as "110 Fill-in-the-Blanks to Knit and Crochet." Of the 110 patterns, 108 of those will be for knitting and only two will be crochet, and one of those two will be ugly. There isn't a crafter in the land who will pay $24.99 for just one pattern, any pattern.

The real reason I think this particular hobbyhorse got started is that so many of the crocheters I have met learned to crochet without learning to read patterns first. Crocheters as a group tend to be very visual. I don't know many knitters that can avoid the siren song of a cool knitting book even if they have just started knitting, whereas I know many crocheters who have been crocheting for years without ever cracking a book—especially if they love to make afghans. I could make a dozen afghans off the top of my head with stitches that I already know and don't really need a book to tell me how to do it. It's the nature of crochet.

A corollary of this "crocheters don't read" myth is that crocheters copy patterns. As in make copies of bought patterns to pass to their friends, thus ensuring that the friends don't go buy the pattern themselves and meaning the publisher, and by extension, the author/designer don't get paid. I don't know that crocheters are any more likely to do this than knitters or if they are just getting tarred with the "cheap" brush again. I do know that if one more person tries to sell me a crochet design that is the same granny square jacket that has been published since 1968 I am going to scream. I do not need to buy a pattern to make a granny square—I have been making them since 1968, myself. Show me something beautiful and innovative, and I will buy it.

Crocheted fabric doesn't drape. Crochet by its very nature has a structural quality—that is one of its best features. Of course, if you make a jacket out of single crochet with a giant hook and yarn the thickness of rope, you will get a sturdy garment with no drape at all. In fact, the boxier patterns out there might serve as storm shelters that stand up on their own if the circumstances demand it. However, use a smaller hook, some DK-weight natural fiber, and an open stitch, and you can wind up with a diaphanous piece of wonderful that clings in all the right places.

Granny squares are the (square) root of all evil. Despite the great amount of time I spend weeding through antique and vintage crochet patterns (pretending it is work instead of procrastination), I haven't quite figured out when the granny square first came about, and if it was called a granny square at that time.

Granny squares are wonderful things—portable, customizable, and the perfect building blocks for items that are square or rectangular. I think the problem came about when the granny migrated from afghans to sweaters—some boxy sweaters are not a bad thing, but millions of them are a bit boring from a fashion standpoint. This does not mean that making granny squares is a bad thing, but that their use should be confined to appropriate projects.

Crochet does not have the history that knitting has. Crochet might or might not have a long and distinguished history, but I don't know because what we don't have is a definitive crochet history book. Most likely, modern crochet didn't get codified until sometime between 1835 and 1845, which makes it an infant in the world history of needle arts. Many early crocheters were imitating the much more expensive and time-consuming craft of making point lace. Thread lace, which went on to turn into dress fronts, lingerie trim, and doilies, eventually migrated into yarn crochet for both home decor items and warm garments such as a sweater. Crochet may not have been around for thousands of years, but because of the large numbers of crocheters on planet Earth, it has developed new branches and forms almost nonstop. The thing about crochet's history or lack thereof is that I don't think most of it has happened yet—the things we do today will inspire the crocheters of the future.

Only old ladies crochet. Actually this last accusation tends to be thrown at both knitters and crocheters by those who aren't capable of doing either. Generally, I just raise my eyebrows at this one and point out that I do not consider myself old. I can't wait until I reach the age where I can just whack the ill-spoken lout with my cane and get away with it.

Crocheting has some real benefits to those of any age—it keeps the mind as well as the fingers agile, and being part of a like-minded community can combat loneliness and stress at any age. When I am an old woman I may not wear purple, but I will definitely crochet with it and any other color I can get my hands on. Hell, I might even relent and make a toilet paper cover; you just never know.

Granny Gets a Makeover

W hy is it that the mainstream media can't resist taking shots at Granny? Every time crocheting gets labeled cool or trendy, someone somewhere, who I am sure thinks that he or she is being very clever and original, says, "This is not your grandmother's crochet!" Like that's a good thing. One of the things I like about crochet is that my mother did it, and my grandmother probably did, too. I personally don't want to disengage from Granny but to take her work and move forward from it.

And what do we as crocheters have named in Granny's name? The granny square. The poor granny square gets mocked from time to time, particularly in reference to some of those boxy, clunky, garment styles from the 1970s.

Granny squares don't need to be changed, but I think they need a little PR. Some clever designers have taken to referring to any sort of repeatable unit, including granny squares, as "motifs." This is a great idea—let the art of the pattern speak for itself without any knee-jerk negative connotations drawn from the name. I probably wouldn't look twice at a pattern called Granny Square Poncho but I would be intrigued by a Square Motif Wrap.

So I propose a new nomenclature . . . instead of being a granny square, a particular motif could be called, I don't know . . . Jenny or Tiffany . . . or Kate. Jenny could be hip and trendy, whereas Granny might be a little old fashioned. Tiffany could be lightweight and drapey, whereas Granny might be a little stiff in the joints. Kate could be sunny and warm without being a mélange of too-bright colors like Granny was in her hippie days. It's the same great square, but a new name that doesn't carry the negative connotations of the past.

I Am Not a Hooker

I don't want to be a wet blanket who takes all the fun out of wordplay, but I have to say, the whole "crocheters are hookers" thing makes me a little nuts. In my own personal opinion (and you may certainly disagree), crochet gets little enough respect in the world at large without calling its practitioners the same name as those who ply their trade at the world's oldest profession.

Why is it that crocheters have to be called anything other than crocheters? Is it the dicey spelling? Is it supposed to make us more palatable to the noncrocheting world? Are there any cutesy names for knitters that I am missing? At the risk of sounding like a bad *Seinfeld* parody, what's up with that?

One yarny magazine for which I wrote wanted to avoid the whole hooker issue and referred to crocheters throughout as loopers. Loopers? That brings up pot holders for me but, okay, at least it doesn't have a pre-existing negative connotation.

Sometimes a group needs to fight for their label in the interest of self-respect. When I worked on costumes in the entertainment industry, I always identified myself as a tailor or a stitcher. But that had a spelling reason. Think for a minute, how do you spell the word meaning one who sews, which is pronounced soh-er? Sewer. How do spell that underground morass filled with waste water, which is pronounced soo-er? See? I want to be confused with a dank underground cesspool even less than I want to be confused with a lady of the evening.

The problem with words that identify a person with one craft or another, is they aren't real helpful for those of us who are multicraftual. Does identifying a person as a crocheter or a knitter (or a spinner or a quilter) mean that they do just that craft and no others? That seems a little limiting to me. That single-craft identifier can lead one trippingly down the primrose path to stereotyping as well—it's easy to make a generalization about a small group if that group is identified as "other." And now I sound like a bad sociology professor instead of a stand-up parodist—sorry about that.

There are a lot of terms describing a practitioner of the world's oldest profession—lady of the evening, streetwalker, escort, hooker—because polite society does not want to come out and say "prostitute," which is what one is talking about. The less descriptive terms make the job more palatable in conversation.

But you know what? I don't think people need to avoid saying "crocheter" in any conversation at all, no matter where it is held, or what age the participants. There is nothing even vaguely shameful about crochet.

So if you must call me something, I prefer author, designer, stitcher, and even the somewhat bulky needlecrafter. I will accept crocheter with good grace, although that is not all that I am. Just please, don't call me a hooker. Not even a happy one.

New Ideas for Enterprising Yarn Store Owners

Today I brought a crochet project along with me on a two-hour flight. It's a lacy openwork in treble crochets, and my hook flew along. The piece in front of me grew at warp speed, and I remembered once again what an instant-gratification jolt I can get from crochet. Luckily the flight wasn't too crowded, as the ball of yarn jumped off my lap and rolled around under the seats from time to time because of the speed with which the yarn moved through my fingers. It was a new design of mine so I fiddled and fooled, occasionally ripping a bit out, only to rework the area so it looked even better. I crocheted, I took notes on the pattern, and I was happy.

Now? Not so happy. Why? I ran through that 220-yard skein of yarn already and all of its cousin skeins are in the checked baggage. I have a ninety-minute connecting flight and nothing to do! Nothing! Why, oh, why aren't there yarn stores in airports? Do we really need 1,500 coffee bars? Couldn't some of that space be used for yarn? There is a freaking children's museum in this acres-wide airport, but no yarn. Somehow, it doesn't seem fair.

Sheer statistics should prove that thousands of knitters and crocheters move through a hub airport on any given day—why should the caffeine dependent be catered to more than the alpaca dependent? And actually, giving more caffeine to certain fliers only makes life worse for those around them, whereas giving yarn to the yarn deprived would make them calm and much more pleasant travelers. So my first vote for places yarn stores ought to open up is in the airport, train station, and, yes, even the bus depot.

While I am fantasizing, the next thing I would like to see is a yarn store that is open during the wee hours of the morning, especially in the weeks leading up to major gift-giving holidays. By the time my daughter and I get through homework, real work, dog walking, dance class, garbage-taking-out, a spot of laundry, wolfing down some food, *and* I have time to sit with my hooks in hand and get some quality time with my crocheting, (a) it is invariably past midnight and (b) I find I am missing some pertinent part, such as the correct size hook or the contrast color yarn. How happy would I be to zip over to a yarn store at 1:00 A.M. to get what I need. In the later hours, I suspect the clientele would primarily be insomniacs happy to have something to do other than worry about the fact that they aren't sleeping. And an open store would be a boon for absentminded last-minute gift finishers who are always short on something with four hours to go. Think of the hundreds of boxes that could be opened on birthdays and winter holidays that would contain actual finished gifts rather than oddly shaped swatches, hooks, and partial skeins of yarn. Holiday joy would increase exponentially for all.

When I get in my more reclusive crafting jags, what I wish for is a yarn store that would deliver. Yeah, I know about Internet shopping and all, but that takes a few days until the fiber is in my hands. What I really wish for is a place I could call up and say, "I need three skeins of 100 percent wool worsted weight in a dark blue," and then someone would bring it by the same day. Maybe the delivery person would bring a couple of different choices, and I could take the one I wanted and send the others back. I would tip for that. I might even want that job—can you imagine the look of delight you would receive when you showed up on someone's doorstep with the yarn she needs? You would be better loved than the ice-cream truck guy on a hot summer day!

The last yarn store idea I think would be cool has actually been attempted in the past, although it seems to me the company I am thinking of disappeared off the face of the earth with barely a splash. Think Mary Kay or Tupperware—home shopping party–plan yarn buying! Instead of a makeover, we party hosts would get the opportunity to swatch with new yarns, and we wouldn't ever have any problems getting our friends to attend. A couple of yarny party games (Name this fiber! Guess what size hook this is!), some refreshments, some shopping, and a good time would be had by all.

Okay, yarn store owners, discuss among yourselves. They are calling my flight. I hope they have some recent magazines or it's going to be a long ninety minutes.

The Center-Pull Skein—
Modern Convenience or Urban Legend?

lthough there is something satisfying about placing a hank of yarn on the umbrella swift and running it through the ball winder until it resembles a slightly fuzzy hockey puck, I am sometimes taken in by the siren song of a yarn that is sold in a center-pull skein. Many manufacturers allege that you can stick your finger into the exact middle of a commercially wound skein of yarn, pull out the end, and start crocheting away—no muss, no fuss. It saves time—you can get right to the crocheting part rather than getting sidetracked by the much less-amusing fiber preparation part. Machines can do everything, can't they? They make these perfect little skeins that make our crocheting lives so much easier. (But think about this, if machines are so darned clever, why can't they crochet?)

What I tend to get when I stick my finger in the exact center of a skein and yank out what I think is the end is a large glob of yarn barf.

Which I then have to sit and untangle, largely eliminating whatever time I thought I was saving by skipping the ball-winder step. Sometimes the barf blob is pretty easy to untangle and tease out into submission. But if it is large, I end up wrapping it around the outside of the skein, again sort of missing the point of the center-pull skein in the first place. Sometimes it takes quite a bit of time to get the tangle out, and I start muttering some very unkind words under my breath—and of course the higher my stress level gets, the worse I get at the gentle art of yarn detangling, making the process take even longer. Sometimes I give up in frustration and start crocheting from the outside end, which makes the skein wobble away or get caught in the project bag as you pull off more yarn. I rationalize that the time spent chasing the skein is less than the time I might have spent untangling the yarn blob. I almost never resort to scissors—I hate knots in my yarn more than I hate wasting time sorting out yarn barf.

If center-pull skeins are so frustrating, why then do I even try? What draws me back again and again, wanting to believe that this time, this time I will reach in, pull out the end, and be crocheting within seconds of selecting the skein from the stash? Hasn't experience taught me anything? Am I a glutton for punishment? Will I never learn? The answer is the rush I get from that rare time, maybe one time in ten, that it does work. I feel so enormously clever when I pull out the start of the yarn on the first try—it's like winning the lottery. Yes, I know that the vast majority of times that I buy a lottery ticket will result in my holding a worthless piece of paper, yet the occasional win of a few dollars keeps me coming back for more. Intellectually, I understand that statistics tell me that I would be more successful rewinding every skein of yarn that I work with, just as I would probably be in better financial shape if I never again bought a lottery ticket but put those couple of dollars a month into some sort of high-yield financial instrument. But playing it safe isn't nearly as much fun. No risks, no reward. No lightning strike of good luck, no rush. So I will continue to walk on the wild side and gamble on the center-pull skein. I am just a rebel that way.

Attention, Drop People Everywhere: Crocheting and Knitting Are NOT THE SAME THING!

My daughter (and sisters, and anyone else who has been in the same room with me and a film or television program at the same time) has gotten quite used to my yelling at the screen every so often when I spot an egregious anomaly. Part of it, I suppose, is due to my odd work history in which I spent a lot of time making costumes for Broadway, film, and television, a lot of time buying and selling vintage clothing and textiles, and then a lot of time designing knit and crochet patterns. Anyway, what is guaranteed to send me right over the edge these days is when a character in some film or television show is supposed to be doing one craft or another and is quite obviously doing something else entirely.

There are people around the world who look for continuity errors for fun (Look! The glass on the table is full! Now it's empty! Now it's full! Now it's halfway! Now it's gone!!!) and post about them on the Internet—my thing has always been costumes. I do not want to see the zippers in clothing that alleges to be three hundred years old. I do not want to see 1960s clothing on a set that is supposed to be in the 1940s. Do your research, people! My particular pet peeve has always been white Lycra tights in films set in the colonial era. I invariably yell something like, "Too white, too fitted, and they didn't have freaking Capezio in 1776!" Not that the characters answer—if they did, that would just be creepy.

I don't remember being bugged by this so much in years past, but now it seems that not a month goes by that I don't catch a crochet/knitting-related jumble onscreen. Perhaps it is because as needlework has had a recent surge of popularity, writers turn more characters into knitters or crocheters. But for God's sake, if they have a consultant on a medical show to make sure the actors don't speak like complete nimrods, even if their standards of medical care would lead to lawsuits and death (not necessarily in that order), would it really blow the budget to check in with a needleworker somewhere and say, "Hey, crocheting . . . is that the thing with one hook or the thing with two needles?"

And I know I am not the only person who notices this stuff. There are umpteen million needleworkers in the United States alone. Was I the only one yelling at a recent episode of *Drake and Josh*, in which a mother and daughter said they were knitting, but the prop department had basically stuck two knitting needles and some loose yarn along the edge of a granny square afghan and the mother sort of flailed it around? Helloooooooooo . . . not only was it not probable, but it was pretty darn ugly!

When I was in the costumers union in NYC, a good friend and I thought it would be a swell idea to offer our services as needlework consultants to film sets. We had experience as both crafters and on-set technicians, so we figured we could supply a range of prop and costume pieces that were actually accurate and save everyone time and aggravation. Need a half-finished sock to put in your character's hand? We could do that. Need a crocheted scarf because the character said she was a crocheter? We could do that, too. We could even go on-set and give the actors enough of a clue about the hand motions so that they could fake their way through a crafting scene . . . although it certainly would be a lot more fun for all of us if they hired crocheters to play crocheters on TV.

I could just see it now. "Okay, Vanna, you are going to crochet throughout this scene to add to the dramatic tension . . . Okay, cut! Vanna, I said CUT!"

"Not until the end of the row, darn it, I will lose track!"

Or, "Hey, Vanna, we are going back to the start of the scene. Rip out the four rows you just did, for continuity please."

"Rip them out? Are you insane? They are perfect!"

Then there is the speed issue. On *Grey's Anatomy*, there was an episode in which a doctor knit and finished a man's sweater in a day, and had time enough left over to wear it for a while, and then give it to her boyfriend. Yes, it was on largish needles, not a complicated pattern, and the character was supposed to be an experienced knitter. But come on, the finishing alone would have taken a good hour and didn't she actually have to go be a doctor for at least part of the day? Seriously? It was kind of cool that the sweater was part of the plot and all, but couldn't it have been at least as realistic as the medicine?

Actually, I think you can tell when there is a dyed-in-the-wool crafter in the writers' room instead of someone who read an article saying needlework was trendy and turned a character into a crocheter. On *The Suite Life of Zach and Cody*, there was a subplot that a rumor was running around the middle school that a romantically involved couple was going to move far away to raise llamas. Every time this got repeated, one of the boys scoffed at the idea "because everyone knows the real money is in alpacas." I still laugh every time I see that episode because I just know a needleworker in the writer's room did the happy dance that week because she got some actual fiber jokes into the show. Good for her, whoever she is.

Oh, and for the props person who might be reading this, crochet is the one with one hook.

Crocheting in the Closet

I have been a devotee of playing with fiber since I was seven years old—and that is far enough in the past that I don't quite want to say how long ago it was. Suffice it to say that I have crocheted, knitted, and needlepointed my way through many swings in any one craft's social perception. I've been steadfast in my refusal to follow the dilettantes who put down their hooks and needles when a craft isn't hip anymore.

Currently, I suffer discrimination when crocheting. However, the perpetrators aren't the ones you might suspect. I have been working on a blanket for Project Linus recently, striped in vibrant blues and greens in response to the local chapter's request for less traditionally girly colors. It is soft, cushy, and bright—and it is crocheted. When I work on it in the waiting room of my daughter's dance class, no one says a word other than to comment on how pretty it is. When I pull it out at the local yarn store's sit and knit night, however, I can see the eyes roll and the teeth grit as soon as it become evident what project I will work on that night.

"That again?" says one woman who has umpteen unfinished knitted things in her bulging project bag. "Isn't that . . . crochet?" says another as she looks down her nose and shudders. Here among my fellow fiber addicts, where I think I should feel completely comfortable in my choice of craft, I feel the sting of rejection. It is as if I have whipped out a cheeseburger and fries in the middle of a vegetarian restaurant. Often I am tempted to stuff the blanket back in my bag and pull out a pair of complicated socks knit on five double pointed needles just to fit in and prove that I am a "real" knitter. And some nights, when I am too tired to buck public opinion, that is just what I do.

In the last few years we have heard all we ever wanted to about knitting. The media blasted the same headlines over and over, "Knitting is the new yoga! Knitting isn't for grandmothers anymore! Knitwear leads the fashion trends!" I knitted when it was trendy and I knitted when it wasn't . . . the only upside that I can see to the media trumpets is that people don't look at me quite so oddly when I knit on the bus.

But I feel on some levels that the knitters jumped onto the cool kids' bus and have tried to lock the doors behind them to keep the other crafters out. Are they so insecure in their newfound societal acceptance that they don't want to muddy the waters? Is there only so much fiber tolerance in the world? Is it really that they can't reliably do a double crochet and are jealous? I just don't know.

I find it especially odd, because at the most basic level, crochet and knitting both are all about fiddling with string to make something beautiful. So why the competition? Why don't people do both? And why do I feel compelled to hide my crochet habit when I am outnumbered? I find myself sneaking *Interweave Crochet* into the bottom of my stack at the local yarn store underneath the knitting magazines. If pressed, I might even blurt out that I was buying it for a friend.

Craft, like medicine, has become increasingly specialized. Years ago, craft magazines catered to crocheters and knitters both, as well as those who did embroidery or needlepoint. There weren't different magazines for each craft. You paged through *McCall's Needlework and Crafts*, or any of the popular women's magazines, and made whatever appealed to you. We weren't neurosurgeons; we were general practitioners—solving whatever problem was put in front of us with the best tools we had at hand.

Like living through other trends, I am trying not to get carried away on the specialist wave. I make what I like, when I like it, and am happy enough to knit or crochet (or weave or spin or needlepoint) if that's what I feel like doing at the moment. I got faked out by the surge of knitterly acceptance and need to get back to my "do what I feel like" roots.

But crocheters, knitters, weavers lend me your ears! Can't we all just get along? I really need to finish that blanket . . .

The World Wide Web of Crocheters

The intersection of craft and technology always amazes me. When you come right down to it, you can't get much less technology dependent than the basics of crochet. You need something stringlike and a bent piece of something (although if you don't have that second item, you could probably get a fair bit of something made with your bent finger). So yarn + implement = craft, and sometimes, = art. It is the human input that makes crochet beautiful. Of course, in a lot of technological developments, human input = operator error. Human quirks are to be avoided rather than treasured.

One of the fine things that science has brought to almost all of us in the last couple of decades is the Internet. Not just the Internet, of course, but all of the tools that make it so easy to zip around cyberspace and communicate with others. We have social networking sites to chat with like-minded friends, shopping sites to buy things we like that would not otherwise be available to us, blogs to read, podcasts to listen to, and streaming videos to watch. We can have all of this information, from the ridiculous to the sublime, right at our fingertips in the privacy of our own homes. Not only do we not have to change out of our PJs to go online, but we can stay completely anonymous if we like. We can each be in charge of how much interaction we desire.

Crocheters, though, like community. We like to hang out with other crocheters, talk about crochet, and examine new yarns and new patterns. Like attracts like, and crocheters around the world are beginning to find one another. And it is good, because no crocheter in the world has to feel like she is alone in her obsession; there are thousands of yarn-addicted folks out there just like her, and she wants to meet them all! Forums, chat rooms, podcasts, photo streams, even videos . . . so much to see! So many people to hear from! More crochet information than she ever knew existed in the whole wide world and at her fingertips!

The problem now is, do you talk about crochet, or do you crochet? Do you get involved in all the heartfelt stories of those who are collecting crochet for various charities, or do you get out your hook, make something for the group you read about last week, and get it in the mail? Should you start the cute sweater that your favorite blogger showed on her blog yesterday, or should you keep searching because there might be something better out there? Should you download every episode of your favorite podcast, or see what the other podcasters are up to?

It's called the Web because one thing leads to another with ease. You might start out in one little corner of cyberspace and after a few minutes (or let's be honest, hours) of clicking, you are led elsewhere. I won't say led astray, because there is no astray here—you are finding more and more fascinating things, so fascinating that it is very difficult to turn off the darn computer and go do something else. Like eat, or sleep, or crochet.

But I am going to tell you something for your own good. Most of that information will still be there tomorrow. And the next day. Archives are magical things and just because you found a cool blogger does not mean that at that exact moment you have to go back five years and read every post she ever wrote in order of date. You can pace yourself on yarn and book reviews and photos. You can't start fifteen things at once, anyway. I wholeheartedly encourage you to discover all the magical crochet stuff that is now online. Just make sure you don't forget to stop and use your crochet hooks from time to time. In the end, all we really need is some yarn and a hook.

Too Pretty to Use

*Y*ou have the whole crocheting-gifts-for-others thing down. You have mad crochet skills and no longer need to stick to rectangular objects. You stalked the happy couple before the wedding to see what their favorite colors were, analyzed the need for dishcloths at your best girlfriend's house (no, she doesn't always use the dishwasher), and checked the preferred outerwear colors of your favorite babysitter. You have taken note of allergies, style preferences, and sizes. You have taken utility into consideration as well as style. You may, in fact, havelearned the lesson that not everyone in the world appreciates a handmade gift, and you have crossed those philistines off your lists. In short, you have crocheted the perfect gift—not just something you had a burning desire to make, but something that was uniquely suited to the recipient.

And you gave it to them. And they reacted perfectly—with appreciation of the time and thought, and dare I say it, even the love that you put into it. Your work here is finished . . . both gift giver and gift recipient are well pleased with themselves and with each other.

Time passes. You are thinking fond thoughts, maybe even planning their next crocheted gift. And yet . . . the afghan remains in the closet, the dishcloths in the linen drawer in the kitchen, the gloves folded neatly on a shelf. "What happened?" you wonder. "This gift was perfect, I know it was." So you wait, and you hint, and you try for patience, and finally you can't stand it anymore so you blurt it out, "What happened to the gift?" "Oh. We still have it," comes the reply; "it's wonderful." "Was it the wrong color? The wrong size? The wrong fiber?" you ask. "Oh, no," you hear back. "Then where in the heck *is* it?" you finally bellow, all semblance of sanity gone. You know you might have gone a teensy bit too far when the recipient backs slowly away from you, but you can contain yourself no longer. How can someone refuse to use something when clearly it is perfect?

Then comes the answer. "It is too pretty to use!" This is the answer from hell because there is no fighting it. They haven't said it is the wrong color, wrong size, wrong fiber, wrong gift. They are agreeing with you that the gift *is* perfect. In fact, it is so perfect that they don't want to use it because, if something happens to it, it will be perfect no longer! They can't put the afghan out because the toddler might spill grape juice on it. They can't use the dishcloth because their dishes are, well, dirty and the cloth might become gross. They can't wear the gloves because they drink coffee on the run every morning and what if they had a spill? They would rather preserve the gift as a museum piece than run the risk of doing your gift damage.

It isn't that they don't appreciate your work (like Uncle Paul who wanted to know why you bothered to crochet him a scarf when he had a perfectly good one from the dollar store). It is that they are *so* appreciative of the work that went into it that these friends of yours would rather deny themselves the pleasure this item might bring them than do it damage. A noble thought, but one that is bound to make you crazy. They think they are respecting your work and doing you a favor.

There is only one way to combat the "It's too pretty to use" excuse, and that is recipient education. Explain to the person that the item was meant to be used—the cotton yarn you used is sturdy for a reason, the acrylic can go in the washer and the dryer, the linen will become softer with use. Explain all the best ways to wash the item if it does get dirty. Explain that the item brings no joy to anyone if it is locked in the closet.

And if that doesn't work, beg. "If you use this gift and it does wear out, I get to go buy more yarn and make another one without guilt! Please use this item, please please pretty please with cashmere on top!" Your recipients are your friends and they want to make you happy, right? This technique almost always works. And if it doesn't, tell them they go on the "buy gift from dollar store" list, right next to Uncle Paul. And no one wants that.

There Is No Wrong Way to Crochet

The other night in a crochet chat room someone asked me if I held my hook in a pencil grip or a knife grip. "I don't know," I replied. "Well, pick up a crochet hook and look," she said; "I am really curious." So I picked up a crochet hook (because there is always one nearby, right?) and made a stitch or two. And I still didn't know which kind of gripper I am. If I tried to hold a pencil or a knife the same way that I hold my crochet hook, I would neither be able to write longhand nor eat. So I pretended I didn't see her question and signed off shortly thereafter. There is an episode of *SpongeBob Squarepants* in which SpongeBob tries to analyze how he ties his shoes, and gets so befuddled that he can't do it anymore. I do not want to forget how to crochet.

I know that I crochet oddly. I know this because I have watched a million other crocheters ply their needles and they never do it the same way I do it. Periodically, I think I should learn to crochet "correctly" and

I will frustrate myself for a few hours trying and then I give up and do it the way I always have. I end up with results that please me, are recognizable as crochet stitches, have a nice even gauge that only comes from thousands of stitches of practice, and so I get over worrying about my odd process. It is what it is.

I take a similar, laissez-faire approach to following patterns. I try, I really do try, to be obsessive and follow every little note and every little detail, but sometimes I can't quite catch what the designer wanted me to do, so I punt. I look at the photo, I look at what I am doing, I have the general gist in my head of what comes next, and so I just do what I think needs done. Is mine going to look exactly like the photo? Maybe not. But it will do what it needs to do, it will be done, and done is good.

Sometimes my crocheted items come out not looking at all like the model in the photo—not because I deliberately chose to flout the instructions, but because maybe I was not paying quite enough attention. I have a wonderful way of rationalizing these kind of outcomes, too. I do not make mistakes—I make design modifications. I modify the pattern to get the results I want. Or at least that's what I pretend I do. In actuality, my criterion for frogging the heck out of something is pretty simple. Is whatever boneheaded thing I did symmetrical, and therefore it looks like it was on purpose, even if it wasn't? Yes? It's a design modification and it stays in.

When I taught drama, I used to tell my students that if they forgot their lines they should just say something that furthered the scene along. "After all," I told them, "the audience isn't following along in the script." I feel the same way about patterns. As long as someone is not coming at me with a pattern in her hands to do a line-by-line comparison between my garment and the text, then it's all good. I will get to the finish line eventually and with most of the plot intact, and 99.9 percent of people looking on won't know the difference.

Finish or Frog, or the Fine Line between WIP and UFO

For those of you who are unfamiliar with the terms, WIP means "work-in-progress," and UFO is "unfinished object." When does a WIP become a UFO? To me the issue is the *P* for *progress*. If no progress has been made in a long time, it's usually either time to muscle through it until it's finished, or rip it out and put the yarn back in the stash until it calls out to be made into something else.

Of course, the definition of *a long time* will vary from crocheter to crocheter. Some folks consider a long time to be a week or two, some measure a long time in months, and I have to admit, I have had projects around for years before I actually did something about them one way or the other.

Most of the time you dig up one of the moldy oldies not because you were looking for it, but because you were looking for something else and it got it in your way. If you greet it like a long-lost friend, more than likely you are going to finish it, and soon. Projects like that can be a real boost to the part of you that requires instant gratification—you can get something done in half the time you would normally take because a good chunk of it is done already. Wow, a new sweater in a week! That is always pretty exciting.

If finding this project makes you cringe, break out in a cold sweat, or run away in fear, for goodness sake, frog the thing so it can't haunt your dreams any longer. There is no such thing as time wasted crocheting. Even if you spent hours on whatever this is, if you are going to hate it when it's over, rip it out and move on. At least you got some good crocheting hours out of it, so don't make yourself crazy finishing something you don't really want anymore. And maybe the yarn would make you happy if it was worked up into something else.

Here are some common reasons that the finish-or-frog question comes into play, and some hints on how to make the right decision.

1. *You find a partially finished baby sweater and the baby is in high school.* This one could go either way. Clearly the intended recipient doesn't need it, but on the other hand, there are always babies needing lovely crocheted gifts. I base this one on this condition: if it has weathered the years well, I would finish it and be prepared for the next baby shower I was invited to. Bonus points on timing if the original baby is now expecting— you can finish the sweater, give it to the newborn, and have a funny story to tell at the shower.

2. *You find what was supposed to be a cute, trendy garment well after the trend has passed.* This, too, is a timing issue. If the trend has recently passed into fashion oblivion, frog it. You aren't going

to want to wear it out in public, and the yarn is probably good for something else. If the trend passed into oblivion twenty years or more ago, you might want to finish it—it's going to come back into style any minute!

3. *It was ugly then, it's ugly now.* Frog it. Life is too short for ugly crochet. We all occasionally make mistakes putting projects together—frog it and forget it. At least there won't be proof of your error in judgment, just some more yarn sitting on the shelf.

4. *The pattern is missing or so poorly written that it made you crazy, which is why it got stuffed in the closet in the first place.* Frog it now before it strikes again! Crochet is supposed to be a leisure activity—sure, it can be challenging, but it shouldn't be something that makes you want to tear your hair out. Destroy this project before it destroys you!

The frog-or-finish question does not have to be settled immediately upon discovering a candidate. Sometimes what you need to do is work a few rows on the piece. If it's fun, finish it. If you smack your forehead and say, "*That's* why I put this down in the first place—what a pain in the rear!" you may now frog with impunity.

I have already acknowledged that I am the type of person that can't throw out yarn, there are some people who can't frog half a project no matter how much they know that even if they finish it they won't be happy with it. In this case, you still have a few options.

1. *Find a crochet buddy in the same situation and trade WIPS.* She finishes yours, you finish hers. It's quite possible that the WIP

that made you crazy will amuse your friend and vice versa, so this one works out great—two FOs for the price of one and no one wants to cry.

2. *If it's wool or another animal fiber, felt it!* Felt the work you did and then turn the felt into something useful. Since you can cut crochet after it's felted without it unraveling, you can turn the piece into anything from a purse or tote bag to a pot holder to a set of coasters. You wind up with something useful without investing much more time into your losing proposition.

3. *Donate it.* I have a wonderful senior citizens' center nearby that will graciously accept UFOs as well as yarn donations. Some of the ladies think it is fun to repurpose a UFO, so there is always someone who is happy to see it.

4. *Develop a taste for free form!* Finish it up if you must, but you don't have to finish it up in the way you first thought you would. Forget the pattern and make it go together whatever way you want it to. The pattern police are not going to come and take you away, I promise. Although the free-formers might come and collect you as one of their own!

5. *For afghans, throw an edging on what you have and call it done.* So what if you intended to make a king-size bedspread but it's only 18 inches square? It's now done! If you can't use it, donate it to a pet shelter or clinic. Many shelters collect smallish afghan parts to put in with a frightened animal to give it something to snuggle up with. Your work will be put to good use.

6. *If you really don't want to finish it, and you really can't bear to frog it, give it to a friend to frog.* When I was in a local yarn store last week, two of the women who worked there were patiently unpicking and rewinding the yarn from a completely finished sweater. The maker hated it when she was finished with it and didn't know anyone it would fit, but couldn't bear to frog it herself. Maybe you have a friend who is ruthless. Or not ruthless, but able to rip out your project because she is not nearly as emotionally attached to it as you are. Let her at it.

No matter what you choose to do with a moldy oldie, you will probably be happier in the long run if you do something with it rather than let it continue to gather dust. And if your project pile goes down significantly, you won't feel the least bit guilty about starting something new!

What's That Again?

My mother tells the tale of her early crocheting adventures in the language of limited yarn choice. There was wool, there was acrylic, and there was cotton. It came in various weights, but those were pretty much her choices. She bought her yarn at the five-and-ten or the discount store, not at the local yarn store. She bought exactly how much she needed for the project she wanted to do (plus one skein for extra in case she ran out), and when one thing was finished, she saved up and bought the yarn for the next. She didn't acquire yarn as I do—it was something you needed, not something you lusted after. Mom would no more collect yarn than she would, I don't know, plastic wrap. There just weren't enough choices to make yarn double as a collectible item.

A few years back I took her to a beautiful yarn store near her home. I had a project in mind and wanted to buy some yarn for it (as opposed to using four of the hundreds of skeins in my stash, but I digress). I still remember the look on her face as she sat there looking around the store at all the colors, weights, and fibers. This particular store is airy and open and extremely well lit, so the cases of yarn look like museum displays—each one containing something more eye-catching than the last. She still didn't buy anything (although I succumbed to some cashmere/merino blend), but she greatly enjoyed the trip.

Her wonder at the huge variety of fibers available got me to thinking about what yarn is made from. The plant fibers are pretty easy to identify—cotton and linen, right? Oops, there's also rayon (from cellulose, which is wood fiber), corn or soy fiber, ramie (which is related to nettles, but as a yarn has no sting), and I guess all those seaweed/kelp/sea silk fibers would be plant based, too. Of course, within the plant family you have a lot of choices between organically raised, organically produced, and traditionally produced items, and dyed or undyed colorways. Still, a plant is a plant.

Then there are the animal fibers. Generally, I think if you can look at a yarn label and get a mental image of the cute little fuzzy animal whose back it came from, you are doing a fine job. Sheep give us wool, but these days wool is indentified in some cases not just as wool, but as coming from a specific breed—merino comes to mind, as does Blue-Faced Leicester, Corriedale, and Rambouillet (actually Rambouillet sounds like it should be the star of a sheepy action film, but again I digress). Then there is angora (the rabbit kind), angora (the goat kind), mohair (also from goats), llama, alpaca (my favorite), and qiviut (which would be my favorite if I could afford more than an ounce a year). Some intrepid folks spin dog hair, but I don't want to buy any of that—I keep thinking the wet sheep smell I get when my minimally processed wool sweater gets caught in the rain is one thing, but wet dog smell would be quite another thing . . .

For some yarns, you get not only the animal breed but also the animal's name. I have some 100 percent Bob in the closet and recently purchased a Josie/Gracie/Bonnie blend. Since I spin, too, I am about to make some Harrison and some Miss Velvet just as soon as I have the time. This is pretty cool because not only can you picture a cute, fuzzy animal, but you can also picture a specific cute, fuzzy animal that you might have gotten to pet.

Even acrylic yarns have gotten into the act with the type of acrylic specified on the label—as if that makes a difference to me. It pretty much doesn't; in my mind acrylic is acrylic no matter what its subspecies. Dralon? Sounds like a villain from *Star Trek*.

But now there are yarns out there that I am not sure exactly what part of the plant or animal family they came from. I have sock yarn with Chitin in it (it comes from shellfish and has some antibacterial properties, but I am not sure how they get fluffy yarn out of hard shells), milk fiber (again, huh?), and I have a skein of yarn sitting right next to me that says 100 percent vinyl, and underneath in small letters, *Yarn not edible*. Okay, it's called Jelly Yarn, but still, would I put this on my sandwich?

Actually, crab, milk, corn, jelly—lunch is not sounding like a bad idea right now. I can crochet a little after I have my snack. But I promise not to eat the yarn—it's too pretty anyway.

The Real Crochet Olympics

Whenever the Olympics come around, one Internet community or another will organize a related craft game where each participant starts a project when the Olympic flame is lit and finishes it by the end of the closing ceremonies. It all works on the honor system—crocheters can choose the project they want to do and award themselves a gold, silver, or bronze medal depending on how close they get to their goal. It's a lot of fun. But it isn't what I want to see.

I want to see a real Crochet Olympics in which crocheters from all around the world descend on some location or another and compete in a variety of tasks. In real time and in real life with cool opening and closing parties and endorsement opportunities—the whole deal.

The uniforms would have to be crocheted, of course. In fact, the uniform design could be part of the competition with points given for style, fit, and durability. There couldn't be any swimming events, though—I know crocheted swimwear is cute and all (on some people, not on me!) but when it hits the water . . . ewwwww.

Anyway, we could have a fiber identification round in which blindfolded crocheters have to guess the fiber content of a given yarn by feel or smell. Bonus points if they can tell one type of acrylic from another. This would be followed by a speed round to see who can crochet fastest, a technical round in which we could see who has the least fudge factor in their patterns (come on, you know we all cheat on occasion), and maybe a round in which crocheters compete to see who can wield the smallest hook with the smallest thread.

There could be a multiday event much like the Internet version in which crocheters from around the world start a project at the beginning of the Games and finish near the end. That could be something large, for instance, an afghan, or complicated such as a lacy fitted garment.

There would have to be a team competition. Teams could be made up of a specialist in each of six subgenres of crochet—thread, filet, Irish crochet, Tunisian, tapestry, and yarn. Plus, of course, a substitute or two in case the worst happened and someone got a hand cramp. The all-around winner would be the crocheter who could successfully complete the prettiest swatch in all six categories, but medals would be given to the highest-scoring individual in each event.

There could also be related events in shearing and spinning. Maybe a sheep to shawl competition in which teams are made up of spinners and crocheters who have to turn a fleece into a wearable shawl in a matter of hours. There could also be competitions in stuffing a stuffed animal, blocking, and felting. Oh, and a contest for designers in which they have to write out readable pattern instructions in a short period of time . . . the possibilities are endless.

Imagine the Olympic village if it were inhabited by crocheters! There would be no infighting—everyone would happily be working on her free-time projects between events. There would have to be yarn stores everywhere, with yarn and needles and books available from all of the participating countries. The village could even have its own currency—the merino instead of the euro.

I would totally watch this on TV, wouldn't you? Who do we talk to about this?

The New Crochet Reality Show

A friend of mine once said she really wished there was a crochet version of *Project Runway*, in which crochet designers had a certain amount of time to face design challenges, and there would be some fabulous prize, as well as the adoration of the masses at the end. Of course, this wouldn't really work because it takes too long to crochet a garment for the camera—we are talking weeks for full garments as opposed to the days that are edited into the hours we see on TV. We can't just whomp something together out of found materials. And if there was a time limit that was hours rather than days long, everything would be made with six strands of bulky held together and worked on a modified plunger handle. Bulky-weight garments have their place in the crochet pantheon, but a whole collection of them probably wouldn't win any design prizes. So sadly my friend has given up on her reality TV fantasy.

My crochet TV fantasy was always that I would wind up on something like *Survivor*. Everyone would be frantically running around trying to improvise shelter and comfortable beds, and I would dash into the forest, clean off a suitably bent-ended branch, and whip up some hammocks and shelter roofing out of the readily available vines and palm fronds. My team would win all the challenges because they would be dry and well rested. In the end, I would win the million dollars and everyone would agree this was the least uncomfortable *Survivor* in history because crochet had saved the day. When I came back, I would sign a development deal with a large eco-friendly yarn company, and palm frond–based yarns would be a big hit with crocheters around the world. The end. Gotta say, odds are this one isn't going to happen, either, not least because my poor-swimming, sedentary, doesn't-play-well-with-others self would be a total washout in the wild except for my mad hammock-crocheting skills.

Maybe we could do one of those shows where fifteen random strangers are locked in a house together for a period of time and whoever comes out at the end with their nerves intact wins. We could have some crocheters, a few knitters, a spinner or three, and maybe even a needlepoint enthusiast. We could play games to compete for stash, earn points for actually finishing anything, and argue about color combinations. Although practitioners of the needle arts are generally pleasant souls, I am sure within days, the dramatic tension would increase with accusations of stash stealing, slurs against one type of crafter by another, and lead to the eventual duel of knitting needle against afghan hook. The crocheter would probably lose for lack of sharply pointed weapons, but she wouldn't care because she had had days of uninterrupted craft time, and she is used to being picked on by the knitters, anyway.

Crocheters couldn't be on a personal appearance make over show, because if the host/stylist tried to throw out one of our crocheted garments claiming it didn't suit the current trends, we would be arrested for physical assault (and convicted because there would be proof of the crime on videotape). However, a *Mission: Organization*–style show has possibilities . . . but I can't imagine a host in the world who has more clever ideas about stash storage than the average crocheter. Although maybe such a person would have some input on the upside of stash storage—all that yarn has to have some insulation qualities, doesn't it? Empirical evidence that we are not indulging in hoarding behavior so much as lowering our energy costs would be welcome to most crocheters I know.

Wait, I have it. We need to go steal a bunch of ideas from the Food Network. Isn't a designer sort of like a chef? We all use pretty much the same ingredients. Be it butter or silk, it's the combination of flavors and use of technique that separates one practitioner from another. If Paula Deen makes it, it is going to start with a stick of butter and a pound of sugar; if I make it, it is going to start with a 4 mm hook and a pound of alpaca. What's the big difference? We could have yarn store crawls where the locally produced yarns are sampled. Check in with indie dyers to see how they do what they do. Or we could have a secret theme ingredient (bamboo! corn!) and see how two champion crocheters approach the creative process—both with technique and style, of course, but with completely different results based on their taste and experience. *Iron Crocheter! Allez crochet!*

Dishcloths—Fancy, Fad, or Failure of Imagination?

Everyone has a type of crocheting she loves to do above all others. But no one takes more crap for her selection than someone who loves to make dishcloths. Even other crocheters pick on dishcloth crocheters from time to time. "Why bother?" they ask. "You can buy dishcloths at the discount store for loose change! And even if you make them with inexpensive yarn, why put effort into making something beautiful that you will then plunge into a festering pool of greasy water?"

But the crocheters of dishcloths just smile and keep crocheting. They know that utility and beauty go hand in hand. They know that the entertainment value they get from the crocheting time is worth the price of the yarn. They know that crocheted dishcloths are actually far superior to the store-bought ones because the texture of the stitches makes them effective scrubbers. They know they are helping the environment on many levels—making things by hand, washing and reusing cloths instead of using throwaway plastic sponges, and using natural fibers such as cotton and linen, which will biodegrade when their useful life is done.

But the list doesn't end there. These clever crocheters know that they can satisfy their need for instant gratification on a near-daily basis if they like, and never run out of different stitches to use. In fact, making a dishcloth is a great way to try out a new stitch or technique—swatches lay around and gather dust but a dishcloth is a useful thing to have after an hour's playing around with hook and yarn. And last but not least, a dishcloth crocheter will never be caught short around the winter holidays by not having a gift to give. If anyone shows up with an unexpected treasure, she can snag one of her newest creations, stick a bow on it, and give a welcome present. And if her friend prefers using a dishwasher to doing her dishes by hand, then it's a facecloth with magical exfoliating properties, rather than a dishcloth!

As a side note, watch out about accepting this sort of gift. Once you get used to using a handmade cloth, you will never want to go back to the dollar store brand. Next thing you know, you will be making some dishcloths of your own despite the potential scorn from your fellow crafters. You, too, will just smile and keep on crocheting for you have seen the light.

You'll Never Walk (or Crochet) Alone

If it's fun to crochet something, and it is, and it's fun to hang out at a fiber event with your friends, and it is, how much fun will it be to have a whole bunch of crochet friends working on the same or similar projects at the same time? This, my friends, is the crochet-along (CAL)—you and a bunch of buddies decide on something you all want to work on, and you do it at the same time. CALs happen on the Internet as well as in real life, so you can pretty much always find one going on that features a technique or project you are interested in doing.

Everything goes a little better with friends, although there always seems to be someone in the group that in your secret heart of hearts you would like to smack, just a little. She gives lip service to the "friendly" part of "friendly competition," but you know that in *her* secret heart of hearts that she is getting way too much joy out of finishing first. You know the type—superhigh achievers who try really hard not to sound as if they are bragging when they achieve the goal of a four-week CAL in four days. Complete with blog posts and photos. And a long lament that now they are finished, what are they going to work on? And you try to take that as encouragement. If she can finish it in four days, surely you can do it in four weeks. But a little part of you has died at the thought that you can never ever catch up.

Some CALs are based on themes and last for a preset time—use as much stash as you can, make as many granny squares as you can, finish as many projects as you can, and so on. These are a lot of fun because you can choose whatever pattern works best for you and not get sucked into making something that perhaps you don't completely love. And for these types of CALs especially, a little competition can goad you into achieving more than you thought possible.

These types of CALs can also be great in regards to those chronic overachievers . . . you actually get to feel a little bit sorry for them. On the single-project CAL, an overachiever got to finish her project and gloat—killing herself for a few days but is then off the hook. On these "who can do the most whatever" CALs, she has to keep going. And going, and going, and going . . . leading to the inevitable CAL for overachievers only: "Who can get carpal tunnel syndrome the fastest?" And no one wants to win that one.

Proudly Multicraftual

Guys, as much as I love crochet, and I do love it, I have to confess that sometimes I stray from the way of the hook. I sew and spin; I play with a *kumihimo* braider and a rigid heddle loom. I . . . gasp! . . . knit, too. In public, sometimes. I have no crafting shame.

I go on and on about knitters looking down on crocheters, because some of them do, and I don't like that at all, and I seem to have a lot to say on the subject (in run-on sentences sometimes), but I also want to say just a word or two about maybe some "other craft" acceptance on the part of the crocheters. Knitters: All crochet isn't ugly. Crocheters: All knitters don't suck.

And while I fully and vocally support the crochet revolution, in which crocheters across the world with hooks in hand peacefully (or stridently depending on our moods) demand respect for crochet, the fact that I like to knit socks should not make me a traitor or a sellout or somewhat less of a crocheter. It just means I like to knit socks.

I do not think that liking to work in one medium takes away from my love for another. My interest in working with my hands is not finite; it does not diminish. My love of craft is not a zero sum game in which working with a pair of needles takes away from my enjoyment of working with a crochet hook. I have room in my heart (if not my stash closet) for all of the crafts I like.

I really don't know how the "war between the crafts" came about. Yet I know that there are those on both sides of the divide who feel very strongly that knitters are knitters and crocheters are crocheters and never the twain shall meet. I remember on my first visit to Charleston some years ago, a friend who had visited the area before pointed out a scenic estate and said it dated from the Civil War. The young man driving, who attended a local military academy, politely coughed and said, "You mean the War of Northern Aggression?" We quickly agreed that that's what we meant (he had the car keys, after all), but it made me think. This man had his opinions on the division between North and South and nothing, not even the passage of a hundred years or more, was going to change his mind.

Which is not to say that I am equating an actual war in which lives were lost to the battle between knitting and crochet. While I consider needlecraft to be a lifestyle choice rather than a hobby, I do get that on a scale of one to global annihilation the divide between knitters and crocheters doesn't amount to a hill of beans in this crazy world. So sometimes I find the vehemence with which one side accuses the other of impropriety to be a bit excessive. No matter how passionate we are about our crocheting, it really is not a matter of life or death if everyone agrees with us. Really.

Actually, stepping away from the crochet from time to time makes me appreciate it more. When I come back after a brief absence (because

I can never stay away for long), I love the hook's flying along even more. Crochet is so speedy, so immediate; the speed with which the ideas in your head turn into fabric on your hook can be mind boggling. I imagine something, and then a few days or sometimes even hours later, there it is in real life. Vision made reality, in record time. But I still like to knit socks . . .

Acknowledgments

Thanks, as always, to my principal cast of K-women: editor Katie Anderson (and her stunt double, Lane Butler), agent Kate Epstein, and daughter Katie Temple, all of whom offer support and words of wisdom (or at least good material) on a regular basis. I don't know why you all put up with me, but I am eternally grateful that you do.

Thanks to crocheters past, present, and future, the quiet ones, the strident ones, and everyone in between. Special thanks to Kim Werker and Vashti Braha, who set me on this path, even though they didn't know it at the time.

Please visit www.hookedforlifepublishing.com/BookPhotos.htm for full-color project photos, and www.GettingLoopy.com for the latest interactive podcast.